Graduating to Adulthood

*Lessons for my
grandchildren,
advice for everyone*

Graduating to Adulthood

Lessons for my grandchildren, advice for everyone

Peter Gravelle

Riverhaven Books
www.RiverhavenBooks.com

To my mother,
for her unconditional love
"When you meet someone,
look them straight in the eye and smile"
Phyllis Irene (Conley) Gravelle
1916 – 2007

Published in the United States by Riverhaven Books
www.RiverhavenBooks.com

ISBN: 978-1-937588-20-5

Printed in the United States of America
by Country Press, Lakeville, Massachusetts

Edited by Bob Haskell

Designed and formatted by Stephanie Lynn Blackman
Whitman, Massachusetts

Table of Contents

Introduction

My wife and I have been married for more than fifty years and have had the pleasure of raising four children, each of whom has given us three grandchildren. So we now have a grand total of twelve grandchildren to spoil. Like every father and grandfather, I would like to see all of my children and all of their children live rewarding and fulfilling lives, full of personal enjoyment and happiness. Nothing makes me so grateful about my own life as the rewarding feelings I experience when members of my family do well. To watch each one as they have found themselves and then to see them adjust successfully to our topsy-turvy world, with all of the give and take we all experience, has been heartwarming. Since my family has been such a constant source of pleasure to me, it seems natural for me to do more to help my grandchildren in their quest to achieve rich and rewarding lives. It occurred to me that sharing some of what I have learned might contribute to that effort.

I feel so fortunate to have such interesting and diverse grandchildren. Know that I love each of you dearly and care about the experiences you will encounter as you make your way through the world. Know that I want all of you to live happy and rewarding lives, rich in personal achievements as well as in your relationships with other people.

I'm tempted to start by promising: "Listen my children and you shall have rich and fulfilling lives. The lessons learned throughout life as described by a father to his sons and daughter." However, I also want to avoid overpromising and under-delivering.

In any event, I guess that as we age we begin to reflect more on our own lives. That leads to thoughts about what, if any, value we have added to our families, friends, and, indeed, to the world. In my case, such reflections are proving to be a sobering exercise. For such self-examination to be worthwhile, you need to be as objective and honest as possible, which is not always easy to do when you are dealing with yourself.

Graduating to Adulthood

Rather than attempt to cover an entire universe of ideas, I have decided to record my thoughts and observations about a limited number of subjects principally focused towards aiding my children and my grandchildren and of course, anyone else who may be interested in reading this book.

Hopefully, my insights and ideas will be useful. My desire is that readers will seriously contemplate the ideas and opinions contained herein. I also hope to impart enough knowledge so that readers will avoid some of the mistakes I have made during my lifetime.

With all the activities, demands and diversions in our lives, it seems we never get enough one-on-one time to convey to the people we love the most, many of the concepts and concerns that are on our mind. Frequently, when time is available, it is difficult to organize one's thoughts without a certain amount of preparation.

To that end, I have written about twenty-two various topics that have defined my life. I call them my "Abouts":

About Background; About Rules; About Fear; About Communications; About Leadership; About Love; About Marriage; About Parenting; About Lifestyle; About Goals; About Wealth; About Investments; About Satisfaction; About You; About Faith; About Emotions; About Mistakes; About Success; About Democracy; About Experience; About People; About Health.

Please read each topic carefully and add whatever insights you may gain to your own base of knowledge with which you observe and deal with the world, both around and within you.

I welcome your questions and comments. I intend to revise this document at some point, so don't be surprised if you someday see a more comprehensive version.

Let me also say at the outset that while my own ideas and experiences have contributed to a significant amount of the material contained herein, I have not personally experienced everything that I have written about. I have read it, observed it, or heard it from other people along the way. Therefore, I can't take credit for being the genesis of everything I have written here. I did, however, think about what I read or saw or heard and consider it important enough to pass it along.

There are a few basic things that everyone should understand about the great adventure called "life."

The first is that life is not always fair, and you will be greatly disappointed if you expect otherwise.

Another great truth is that you are unique – one of a kind – in the universe. There never has been and likely never will be anyone exactly like you. You are a snowflake in the history of mankind. While it may at times be advisable to emulate someone you admire, remind yourself of your own individuality and the strengths that only you possess.

Also, unfortunately, there are no "fairy godmothers" or "magic wands" that you can employ on your behalf, although that may appear otherwise when you observe some people who seem to live charmed lives. Furthermore, for most of us, there are no rich parents or grandparents to help us along. Therefore, you have to make your own way, and realize your own dreams and aspirations, by relying primarily on your own skills and initiatives. The more you concentrate on a single objective, the more likely you will accomplish your goals in life and achieve the outcomes you desire.

Just as a magnifying glass can be used to concentrate the sun's energy to start a fire, so you too can set your world afire by staying focused. And always remember that being born and raised in the United States of America is an enormous advantage when it comes to your ability to pursue your ambitions.

A further basic truth about your world is that your life and your future are largely determined by the value judgments you make and the actions you take based on those values.

No matter who you believe is responsible for causing you to be in a given place or situation, it is you, and you alone, who is responsible for your destiny. You are responsible for taking the initiatives to bring about change. You owe it to yourself, and frequently to others, to take ownership of the rest of your life from that point on. You cannot blame others for your past mistakes or bad judgments, because you do in fact have the power to control your own life. You have always had that ability.

Also, bear in mind that God issues you only one body. It's the one you were born with. It is very important that you provide that body with proper maintenance at regular intervals during your lifetime. Treat it like it's your prized possession; because it is! And remember, when you were born you were fully equipped with a brain and all of the necessary software to operate it. It, too, requires proper maintenance and motivation as well as periodic educational upgrades. Both body and brain are fueled by continuous mental and physical exercise.

I feel I am qualified in many ways to comment with authority on the subjects covered in this book. I have known both rural and urban poverty firsthand, and I've shared in the lifestyle of the wealthy. I have experienced mental, menial, and manual labor. I have traveled the globe extensively. That has enabled me to observe the great diversity in the world and mingle with people of many races, cultures and religions.

Financially, I have earned many millions and lost many millions, just as I have made some very good decisions and some very poor decisions. It is a fact of life that smart people sometimes do dumb things. My life has indeed been a great adventure, not without pain and suffering, but always filled with love, joy and expectation. It has been my great privilege to live during a time of profound change – when quantum leaps are being made in so many fields of human endeavor.

My life has not been a straight path. It has rather been the meandering path of a person who possesses a curious nature coupled with a short attention span and a willingness to take risks. However, I have always been an enthusiastic observer; always inquisitive about people, places and things; and always trying to learn from what I have observed – even though I did not always understand what I was witnessing at the time. You could say I have banged around a lot, learned a lot, forgotten a lot, been damaged and repaired a lot. It has, by and large, been a full, rich and rewarding life. And from all of it I have learned lessons that I sincerely hope will help you.

Please allow me one last comment about this book: I hope you will read it carefully and take it seriously. Because I am trying to pass on lessons I have learned, urge you to avoid similar mistakes, and suggest ideas that I hope you will consider, the tone may sometimes seem condescending or pontifical rather than merely informative. Please excuse my choice of words if that is the case. Consider the substance, not the form.

About Background
Learning through a life of extremes and change

Who am I to be giving you advice and counsel about your life? It does matter, doesn't it? You are certainly entitled to know something about what qualifies me to advise you.

I was born January 28, 1938, in Fitchburg, Massachusetts, when a great economic depression was causing considerable turmoil for the United States and the entire world. Imperial Japan was already at war in Manchuria, and Germany was well underway with preparations to invade her neighbors. My father was unemployed at the time of my birth as were many others of his generation. The worldwide economic chaos had started with what is known as the "crash" of the stock market in 1929, and the Great Depression that followed would continue for several years before the even more tragic events of World War II transpired.

My mother had graduated from Fitchburg High School in 1934 and married my father in 1936. My father, who was one of eleven children, had lost his mother to cancer when he was just thirteen or fourteen and I understand, had quit school after the sixth grade to help support his family.

In 1938, America had just one-third of the population it has now, and fifty percent of our people lived on farms compared to less than four percent today. So it was a very different world from yours that I grew up in. I was only three when Japan attacked Pearl Harbor and America entered the Second World War. Some of my earliest memories are about that effort on the home front. I recall air raid drills and stomping on metal cans to flatten them, then helping my mother tie them up with string and put them on the curb for collection so, I learned later, they could be recycled for war production. I also remember my mother using stamps at a small general store to purchase things like sugar and flour that were being rationed during the war. Butter, like so many other things, was just not available.

When Germany surrendered in 1945 it was called VE (Victory in Europe) Day. I was seven, and I remember how excited everyone was. Church bells rang and rang, horns were blowing everywhere, and everyone was on Fitchburg's Main Street singing and dancing and drinking beer and whiskey and celebrating all night long. A few months later came the first atomic bomb followed by a second which was followed by the surrender of Japan and VJ (Victory over Japan) Day. There was more celebrating, but I don't remember it being as loud or as exciting as VE Day.

We lived on Hawes Street in Fitchburg when I was born and subsequently moved to Rollstone Street, then to the corner of Albee and Newton Streets. We next lived on Douglas Avenue before moving to a small farm on Mulpus Road in Lunenburg. From the small farm we moved to a larger dairy farm on Massachusetts Avenue, living with another family that owned the property. Some of my fondest childhood memories are of farm life.

Small farming in Lunenburg was a primitive existence. We lived in just three rooms with a small covered porch. We had a well for water, an outhouse for a bathroom, a single kitchen sink for washing everything that needed washing – from dishes to people – and a small cast iron wood stove for heat. We had no furniture. Our chairs were orange crates. Our beds were mattresses laid on the floor, one for girls and the other for boys. You may find it strange that, given the circumstances, I remember my childhood being fun-filled and happy. It was all I knew, and I delighted in it.

Somewhere around 1950 we moved from the farm to Burke Street in the Whalom district of Lunenburg where my parents subsequently lived out their lives. I left the house when I was twenty-one, in November 1959, when I married a girl named Mary Angela Posco, your grandmother. She was working at Safety Fund National Bank as a Burroughs bookkeeping machine operator earning thirty-nine dollars a week, while I worked at Benjamin Electric Supply as a counter clerk for thirty-eight dollars a week. The cash gifts we received for our wedding paid for our honeymoon, a one-week tour of Civil War sites. We traveled in my new father-in-law's 1956 Oldsmobile. When we returned, we were flat broke!

Mary and I rented a small one-bedroom apartment at 356 Rollstone Street in Fitchburg. That's where Diane was born. After a few years we purchased a small two-bedroom camp on Natick Street in the Whalom district of Lunenburg, directly across the street from my parents' home. The camp was built on blocks, with no cellar, and had a wood stove for heat. We bought it for about thirty-five hundred dollars. The price was right!

We had an oil-fired, hot-water baseboard heating system installed as well as a hot water tank. We were in heaven.

Still, I was twenty-three years old, married with a child, working in sales on a straight commission, and living in near poverty. I realized that if I didn't make some changes everything would stay the same. My way out was education. I knew I had to go back to college. I got accepted at Clark University in Worcester, Massachusetts. I had been unsuccessful at Fitchburg State immediately after high school, so I could only get into Clark's evening program on probation. That meant I had to get B's or better and that I could take only two courses at a time. Over the next two years, however, I did well enough to work my way up to taking five courses each semester. I was attending classes five nights a week and working full time as the office manager at Acme Electric in Leominster for one hundred dollars a week. Meanwhile, our family was growing from one to two to three children and ultimately to four.

I received my bachelor's degree in business administration from Clark University in 1966 when I was twenty-eight and entered the four-year evening program at Suffolk University Law School in Boston. I was awarded my law degree in 1970 and was admitted to the Massachusetts bar in April 1972. I had majored in accounting at Clark because I had reasoned that numbers are the language of business. It was a good choice because I did well in the accounting field. By the time I graduated from Clark, I was the controller for a small paper manufacturer, Romar Tissue Mills, in Wheelright, Massachusetts. I took a position at the Raytheon Company in

Andover after my first year at Suffolk. Raytheon promoted me to manage its worldwide internal auditing staff five years later. I moved up to corporate headquarters in Lexington, Massachusetts.

The job required extensive domestic and international travel, which led to an important decision affecting my life with your grandmother. I resolved to take her with me whenever I traveled to distant places or for extended periods of time. She would be my traveling companion as well as my wife. Obviously, such a practice had an enormous impact on our limited financial resources. However, I made the decision for several reasons, the most significant being my concern for the long-term effects on our marriage.

Like my mother and father, I tend to be extremely loyal to people who are loyal to me. For many years I had left the house early in the morning, taken our only car, gone to work, gone to school, and returned late in the evening. I left your grandmother at home to take care of Diane, Peter, David and Jason. She rarely complained, and she always supported my efforts to advance my career and improve our lives. Therefore, it seemed to me that since there was already a seven-year difference in our educations, my worldly travels could very well create a gulf of life experiences between us that we might not be able to bridge. Other than our family and home, we could have fewer and fewer things in common. It didn't seem fair that I should return from six weeks in Europe and describe to everyone the great adventures I had experienced without your grandmother. She would have to listen to my stories like everyone else.

During the first three years that I was head of Raytheon's internal auditing staff, we spent nearly fifty percent of my earnings on Mary's travel. But we have been sharing the fruits of those journeys ever since. It has given her the confidence to deal with people from all walks of life without fear or intimidation. She has been there, done that! Travel is indeed a great equalizer.

After ten years at Raytheon, I spent six years at Tyco International in a number of financial and management capacities. It was a great opportunity for me to compare business management procedures because, whereas Raytheon had a centralized management operation, with more than five hundred people in the corporate office, Tyco was completely decentralized with only twenty-three people in its corporate headquarters. Joseph S. Gaziano, the CEO and chairman of the board, believed that both responsibility and accountability for the operating divisions resided with the general manager of each division; and that only such functions as corporate leadership, investor relations, tax reporting, and cash management belonged in the headquarters. Gaziano believed his job was to ensure that the right people were sitting in the general managers' chairs.

My time at Tyco International was followed by seven years with Eaton Corporation, again in a variety of financial and general management positions; and by seven more years at Kysor Industrial as vice president and chief financial officer, executive vice president and chief operating officer and, finally, as president. I was also a member of the Kysor board of directors during that entire time. Kysor was acquired by others in February 1997, and I chose to start Family Choice Mortgage and to also become more involved in my longtime love – aviation.

During all of that time, I worked my way up through all of the levels of middle management and into top management, gaining enormous experience along the way. My experience was not limited solely to business practices, but to the behavior of people, their cultures and mores. After touching and feeling more than fifty countries, seeing their people, observing their business practices, and learning how they manage their family and social affairs, I feel privileged to be a citizen of the world and to be able, to feel required, to pass on to you some of the things I have learned.

About Rules

A little rule change can make a huge difference in results

Have you ever wondered about rules? Are they all necessary? Who makes them? Why do you have to follow them?

Remember when you were young? How your parents and sometimes other grownups would tell you "no" when you were doing something, or sometimes when you were just thinking of doing something? Then as you got older it seemed that everywhere you went you were told about new rules for everything. How to dress. What to say. What you could or couldn't do with your friends.

There are rules for school, rules for church, rules for visiting, even rules for playing. Lots of rules! And it just keeps getting worse. Learning to drive, working, going out to eat. You are expected to follow the rules everywhere. And of course we have what is called "the rule of law." All of these rules are meant to maintain order in our society. It is what we call civilization.

My parents and grandparents were strong believers in following the rules and obeying the law and, of course, "minding your manners." It was a core of values that they passed on to me, and I in turn made every effort to pass it on, by word and deed, to your parents who have since passed those values down to you. I'm sure you know what I'm talking about.

As I got older, I began to observe a few things about established rules and the making of new ones. First, I noticed that every time something unpopular or embarrassing happened, our lawmakers or agency heads or school principals created new laws or rules to prevent a recurrence. Seldom are old rules eliminated when new ones are added. That very same behavior can be seen in business and social organizations. It is known as "closing the barn door after the horse has run away." It is a normal human reaction. People do not want to be criticized for making the same mistake twice.

From those experiences I realized that in a democracy especially, but in just about all organizations – from a condo association to a powerful nation – as new rules are added the organization becomes less and less free for the individual members. Society becomes more restrictive as time goes by and the number of people increase and the rules multiply. History is full of examples.

People who first settled in the western United States were very independent and did pretty much what they wanted. It was the Wild West. We read stories about the mountain men who roamed about the mountains virtually unseen for months and even years at a time. But as more people came, they made new rules about what was theirs and what was someone else's. First the Native Americans experienced the effect and were pushed off their land by ranchers and farmers who in turn were often shoved aside by people with mining or oil interests or by expanding communities. Some areas of our West are still known for their independent natures, but that is a relative situation.

As you get older, you will discover there are other reasons why we have so many rules. For instance, establishing rules is a preferred way to separate one group of people from another. Rules are used to give preference to one ethnic group over another, or to grant privileges to some people but not to others. From the racial discrimination that resulted from slavery to tax laws that favor a few, many rules have been established for purposes other than serving the public good, maintaining order, or avoiding embarrassing situations.

Business leaders I know talk about "opportunity through legislation." They diligently seek ways to change a law or regulatory ruling so it will benefit them financially. These people quite aggressively engineer the desired modifications to the rules to get the results they desire. They are seeking some advantage that can be exploited in their favor. They know from experience that a small change in the rules can yield a significant financial payoff for them. This is what most lobbying efforts are designed to do. It is so important to the achievement of profit and success that many companies actually spend more on lobbying governments than on paying taxes to them.

If you examine every major accounting or legal firm, you will find they employ a cadre of people whose sole purpose is to find ways around existing rules and regulations, modify them, or create new ones to benefit their clients. Large businesses do the same, and not just to obtain tax advantages. I read recently that General Electric employs nearly one thousand tax attorneys. They are not on the payroll to simply interpret tax laws but to search for potential changes that, if enacted, would profit the company. Furthermore, they will actually draft the proposed legislation.

This practice is commonly called "looking for loopholes." In reality, it is just as often focused on creating loopholes. As a result of all this time and effort, many large companies, wealthy individuals, or special interest groups have benefited from discovering these loopholes.

How does a new law or rule come about? At our federal and state levels, the usual process goes something like this. A group or individual will come up with an idea that they feel will benefit them. Then they look for a way to champion their cause. These advocates or special interest groups are often involved in the political process on an ongoing basis, contributing to candidates, supporting some causes, and most often employing professionals such as lawyers and lobbyists to advance their agendas. Many companies have public relations departments. Companies make PR part of their business because it is good for business. These advocates are very adept at working the system and persuading the public. Both regulation and deregulation are prime examples of opportunity through legislation. The object is to increase the regulations for your competitors and to change or reduce regulations for your own business.

Defense contractors have refined opportunity through legislation to an art form. When bids are requested for major programs such as new aircraft, ships or other weapons systems, prime contractors seek out subcontractors based on their geographic locations so that a majority of key senators and congressmen will have job opportunities in their districts. The lawmakers will therefore be susceptible to pressure from their constituents to support the bills that provide the required funding and contract awards to the prime contractor. *Aviation Week & Space Technology* magazine reported on an example of this practice on July 20, 2009. Reporter John M. Doyle described, in an article titled "Collision Course," how defense contractor Lockheed Martin "has parceled out F-22 manufacturing to 1,000 contractors in 40 states, making it politically difficult for lawmakers to vote against more Raptors."

Thus, laws are all too often passed requiring the armed forces to acquire equipment they may not need or want. Defense contractor behavior supports the idea that those with the most to gain are the primary advocates of change, which is usually presented to the public as being best for the public good, protecting the consumer or, in the case of defense contractors, "maintaining a strong defense" and helping the economy by creating jobs.

It should be noted that the United States spends as much on defense as all the rest of the countries in the world combined. By comparison, the British Empire at the height of its power spent only about as much on its military as the next two closest countries at the time. We spend more on "intelligence" than the Chinese spend for their entire military. Studies have repeatedly shown that there are many spending options available to the country that actually create more jobs than does the money spent on defense. Jobs created by funding for building and maintaining bridges and highways and other types of infrastructure immediately come to mind. The creation of jobs, however, is usually cited as a major benefit for approving defense contracts or programs.

Often a company or an industry will sponsor a massive public campaign to try to persuade voters that it has the public's best interests at heart. Of course, in the end, that industry seems to be financially well rewarded for its efforts on behalf of the public. It has been my experience that industrial advocates frequently cloak themselves in non-threatening facades, such as "clean coal," that appear to support programs or policies that favor the public when, in fact, they are attempting to destroy or undermine the public good because it does not serve the best interests of the industry. It is called putting the best face on an ugly situation.

When it comes to establishing public policy, advocates know they always have one strong ally – a disinterested and generally uninformed public. That means people like you! Special interest groups need not worry about telling the truth if they know the facts do not concern the people who matter. Their objective is to fool most of the people most of the time.

One of my law school professors lectured over and over again that the best way to beat the IRS in a tax case is to introduce reams of tax codes and regulatory language, the more conflicting, confusing and difficult to understand the better. The people on the jury would in all likelihood become confused and tired of listening to it. Then, my professor admonished, ask the jury how the client, who lacked experience or expertise, was supposed to understand it all. That is the same principle used on voters in elections. Confuse them and they will get sick of listening to everything – including the meaningful dialog. Remember, advocacy groups and businesses employ these tactics because they work!

So it has come to be, in business and politics, that playing by the rules for many people essentially means changing the rules to suit their own purposes. With government, there is always some interest group behind every proposed change. Frequently, parties interested in changing the rules will actually draft the proposed change and then ask a friendly legislator to introduce it or tack it onto an existing bill. They make it easy for legislators to say yes. For example, the Associated Press reported in November 2009 that supporters of tough US sanctions against the Cuban government had given $10 million to congressional campaigns during the previous seven years. The story was based on a report by the Washington-based non-profit Public Campaign that said its study showed how large sums of money from a small group can influence lawmakers. "Perhaps it's the age-old story of money and politics, but 18 members switched their votes on the subject, some in very close proximity to when they got donations," Public Campaign spokesman David Donnelly told the AP.

Robert Pear of *The New York Times* reported in November 2009 how the biotech company Genentech had lobbyists draft one statement for Democrats and another for Republicans who were debating healthcare overhaul. Both statements, under the names of different members of Congress, were published in the *Congressional Record*. Mr. Pear reported that Genentech estimated that twenty-two Republicans and twenty Democrats picked up some of its talking points and that one, Democrat Bill Pascrell Jr. of New Jersey, said he "did not know where [members of his staff] got the information from."

Then we have the case involving a California law supporting minority candidates for local offices. The Associated Press reported in November 2009 on a new law, written by two lawyers, making it easier for lawyers to win financial judgments by claiming that minorities were shut out from running for office; and if the cases are thrown out the lawyers are shielded from any liability. The two lawyers who wrote the bill were linked to every single suit filed at that time and had already collected or billed local governments $4.3 million. Another example of good government working for the people – both of them.

Your government is somewhat analogous to a top, wobbling back and forth on its center point as it spins around. The only thing that keeps your government from spinning out of control is that for every group trying to push it one way, there is another group trying just as hard to push it in the opposite direction: green organizations versus pollution generators; defense contractors versus healthcare interests; business versus labor. They don't always balance out, but for the most part the opposing forces have kept things wobbling around the middle. It's the only thing that saves us.

All of this is to help you understand that some rules are good, some are not so good, and some are just plain wrong. You have to decide which rules should be followed and which should be challenged or changed. Why is someone trying to change something? What does that seemingly innocent adjustment or change of language accomplish? You have to be alert to who is promoting or enforcing the rules and why. So please think about the rules around you. You may even decide it is necessary to promote new or changed rules yourself.

Too often, corruption and greed are richly rewarded because voters are not diligent enough about their responsibility to stay informed. One of the founding principles of the United States of America is that its citizens remain alert and recognize they have a major responsibility to ensure that the real power continues to rest in the people and that the roll of their government is to serve all the people, not just a privileged few. That whole assumption rests on willingness by our citizens to sacrifice their own special interests and to serve the interests of all of our people.

About Fear
Rattle your cage and overcome your fears

I know of no emotion that limits our progress more than our own fear. Each of us tends to exist within a self-constructed cage of fears. It is a cage that we have meticulously and consciously built around ourselves over time. Fear is something that you learn as you grow. When magnified by your imagination, your fears can become much worse and result in genuine problems.

Babies and young children seem to have little or no fear, but they learn to be fearful by doing things that cause older people to yell at them, or they fall off a chair or bump their head or touch something that is too hot or too cold. By the time they reach adulthood, they have what can be described as an extensive stable of fears. Some are based on experience, some on opinions, and many on things they imagine.

If you are going to be happy and enjoy your life, you have to understand your fears. Learn how to recognize them and how to tame them or overcome them instead of living with constant fear and worry. You need to break out of your cage.

Our greatest fear is probably the fear of change because of the unknown element involved. We all seem to get comfortable with the status quo. Why rock the boat? We think we would like to change things, but we continuously ask ourselves: "What can I possibly do?" We constantly invent excuses to justify our lack of will to change. "I would like to go out and have fun more often, but no one asks me." "I would like to learn to do that, but it's just too hard for me." "I'd like to apply for that job, but I know I don't have enough experience."

Anytime you hear yourself saying "but," it's a dead giveaway. You are afraid of something! You want to stay in your cage! It's nice to still have your blankee, isn't it? It means you are more comfortable dealing with what you know than trying to change. Are you afraid someone will tell you "no" or otherwise reject you or your idea?

Another one of our fears is what other people think. "What will they think if they see me doing this?" "How do I look?" "What if so-and-so finds out?"

Instead of giving in to those fears, stop and think. Why do you care what other people think? Are you going to let other people tell you what you can do? If you want to do something and it's not illegal, don't let other people stop you. If it is illegal, you might want to think twice before proceeding, or perhaps you need to try to change the rules. Go back and read "About Rules".

Another way fear can manifest itself is procrastination. Most of the time when you tell yourself you are not ready to do something because you lack adequate information, you are really just afraid to take action or commit yourself. So you avoid doing anything at all or put off making a difficult decision. You will face your fear at another time – maybe.

When I was in high school I learned that personal courage can overcome fear with the result that all other fears are diminished as well. You might say I had my own Outward Bound experience.

Southern New Hampshire has many abandoned quarries that are filled with water. Those old quarries were favorite swimming holes for the adventurous when I was young. Most were located in remote places and were usually surrounded by woods. A newly-found favorite of my classmates was very deep with very cold water. High sheer cliffs were on three sides. I was not familiar with that particular quarry, but when my friends described the cliffs and said they had climbed halfway up and jumped into the water, I asked why they didn't just dive from the top. They explained the cliffs were far too high for that. I foolishly told them I would do just that.

My classmates insisted on taking me up to the quarry because they all wanted to see me do what I had said I would. So off we went. We hiked through the woods to the quarry, arriving on the one side that was almost at water level at its lowest point. My friends pointed out the small ledge that some of them had jumped from, about halfway up the high cliff on the opposite side. It looked to be a long, long way up!

A narrow path led from where we were standing around one side and up to the small ledge. From there, an even narrower path led to the top of the highest cliff. As I climbed towards that narrow ledge alone, I regretted getting myself into this situation. The cliff was much higher than I had imagined. When I got to the ledge, I was still only about halfway up the cliff. I figured the top had to be at least sixty feet above the water.

As I continued to climb, I became very frightened by the height. I thought of all kinds of excuses I could make so I would not have to dive off that cliff. A few of my truly good friends yelled up at me that I really didn't have to dive off the top. It was foolish! It was far too dangerous! Finally, mostly because of my pride, I resolved that the best way to face this was to climb to the top and immediately dive off before my fear overcame me. I did exactly that.

I felt sheer terror when I saw how far down it was to the dark water as I dove from the cliff. It seemed forever before I hit the water. The force yanked my arms back, and pain shot through my whole upper body. The impact knocked the wind out of me, and I plunged deep into the water.

For a long moment I wondered if I could make it back to the surface alive. Then I burst out of the water, gasped for a deep breath of air, and heard everyone hooting and hollering. I immediately acted as if it was nothing at all, and I never let anyone know how really afraid I had been. It had taken all the courage I could muster to make that dive, and the feelings of elation and accomplishment were incredible. It is exhilarating when you overcome your fear. I learned that personal courage can indeed be richly rewarded in the end. Memories of that experience gave me the incentive to overcome many of my future fears.

Death is, perhaps, the fear that haunts us the most. We are afraid of getting old. But we fear dying even more, even though some people believe that the sole purpose of being born is to die.

I'm told that I momentarily died on November 12, 2007. My heart stopped but was quickly started again by an emergency medical technician in an ambulance on the way to a hospital in Abington, Pennsylvania. All of this was the result of an accident during a training session in a centrifuge when I was preparing to become one of the world's first civilian astronauts. It preceded a week in intensive care because of a tear in my esophagus. I lost about eighty percent of my blood in about ten minutes.

At first, during my conscious moments, I felt severe pain, as if someone was trying to rip out my stomach. Then my body went into what I surmise was shock – or maybe I was drugged. As I was wheeled into the emergency room, I was making surreal observations about what was happening. I was only dimly aware of my surroundings and what was being done to me. I knew that at one point many people were performing a number of different procedures on me all at once. Then I went completely blank.

If I hadn't woken up a day or two later, I would never have known the difference. After I did come to, I thought: "Hey, dying is actually easier than being born, and your memory of it is about the same." That near loss of life turned out to be a life-changing event for me because I overcame my fear of dying for good. I learned firsthand that our bodies have a built-in defense mechanism to effectively deal with trauma.

I'm luckier than most. I've experienced almost everything you can do in life, including dying. When you survive an experience such as I had, you gain a new respect for the competency, dedication and devotion to the well-being of others that the people in our medical community bring to their profession. I believe that in my case they truly were miracle workers. They are frequently in my thoughts, and I shall always be grateful to them.

As an aside, let me tell you to never fear talking to me about my death when my time does finally arrive or about my illnesses or whatever else may happen to me as I grow older. Understand that I fully expect to live for at least one hundred years, but I am quite philosophical about it all. I have already outlived most of my high school and college classmates and have been blessed with a happy and most interesting existence. I fear not! That is why I urge you to rattle your own cage once in a while and deal with your fears.

Never feel intimidated! Be decisive! Shake off the fears that surround you and get on with your life. It can be everything you hope it will be and, possibly, some things you could never have imagined!

As Plato noted: "We can easily forgive a child who is afraid of the dark. The real tragedy of life is when men are afraid of the light."

About Communications
Communicating means being understood

The Raytheon Company maintained what was called a Skills Inventory File at its corporate office in Lexington, Massachusetts. It is my understanding that this file was developed by Harold Geneen when he was the company's chief financial officer before moving on to gain fame for his financial acumen as chief executive officer of ITT. The financial controls he left behind at Raytheon were subsequently improved and were recognized among professional audit and regulatory experts as being world class.

Every few years, all accounting, treasury and financial employees were asked to complete a questionnaire that was reviewed with their supervisors and then forwarded to the corporate office for inclusion in the Skills Inventory File. The employees were then categorized according to their skills and experience. I had originally been hired as a cost-accounting supervisor at the Andover, Massachusetts, facility that was part of Raytheon's Missile Systems Division. Within five short years, however, I had been promoted to manage one financial department after another and eventually had about half of the Andover financial operations reporting to me. Because of the success of the Hawk missile system, Andover grew from thirty-five hundred to about eight thousand employees during that time.

One day I received a call from Peter DiAngelo, the controller who was my boss, requesting that I go to his office because he had something important to discuss with me. When I got there, Peter informed me he had talked with someone from the corporate office and that they wanted to see me the next morning in Lexington. He explained that corporate headquarters was seeking someone to manage the company's worldwide internal auditing staff, and they wanted to talk to me about the job because the Skills Inventory File had identified me as having most of the attributes necessary for the position.

I told Peter I was very happy right where I was, thank you, and therefore had no interest in heading up any corporate auditing staff. He then said the interview was something of a command performance, my background had been verified, the division staff had already agreed to it, and I needed to go. If I didn't, it would be an embarrassment for him. On the other hand, Peter said he really hoped I could remain on his staff. He suggested that if I felt strongly enough about staying, perhaps I could not do so well during the interview. In any event, he asked me to see him when I returned from my corporate visit.

Three people interviewed me separately at the Lexington corporate office the next morning. The third interview ended with lunch in a private dining room filled with very impressive looking gentlemen. Then I returned to Andover.

My boss was rather excited when I saw him. He told me he had received a call from his boss's boss who indicated that he and the other interviewers were quite impressed with my demeanor and responses to their questions. I had been selected as one of five finalists. The others were two internal candidates and two external candidates currently employed at big-eight CPA firms. Another round of interviews whittled the five down to me and one of the other candidates. Then I was named to the position.

After initially thinking I would prefer to remain in Missile Systems, I reconsidered my career alternatives and instead chose to move to the corporate office. I was greatly influenced by a friend and colleague at Missile Systems who convinced me there were more interesting and challenging future options by making the move to corporate.

Raytheon operations were worldwide. Company businesses consisted of broad-based domestic and international units, serving commercial as well as government clients, and included both service and manufacturing businesses. I was able to visit almost every division located in countries around the globe including places like Saudi Arabia where tourists were not welcome. I was introduced to a whole new world of peoples and cultures that transcended mere differences in geography. It became in every sense a life-changing experience for me.

After I had managed the internal auditing staff for some time, Bill Pultz, the man who made the final decision on my appointment, told me why I had been selected rather than the other finalist. He explained that it had been a very close call because both candidates possessed similar experience and both appeared to be an excellent fit regarding the position's technical requirements. In the end, the one thing that gave me an edge was the fact that while we each had graduate degrees, and the other person had an MBA from a top-tier business school, I had a law degree. Bill assumed that meant I was more skilled with written communications. Since the manager of Internal Audit was required to issue written reports that would be reviewed by the chairman of the board of directors, the chief executive officer, as well as members of the Audit Committee, it was quite important that all internal audit reports be well-crafted. The educational combination of accounting and law had served me well. Lesson learned: Keep your options open.

Managing Internal Audit at Raytheon proved to be one of the biggest opportunities of my career, and I got the job because others thought I had mastered the art of written communication!

I was thirty-four years old when I learned just how important it is to be able to communicate effectively. By then I had developed some oral communication skills as a volunteer lector in my church and as an elected official for the city of Fitchburg, Massachusetts.

What I learned in my thirties about the role of effective communication you would be well-served to learn as early as possible, hopefully by the time you graduate from college.

This brings me to the challenges you will face in pursuing that goal.

First you must understand that it is truly necessary!

No matter what you choose to do in your life, it is almost certain you will not do it in isolation. You need information from other people, and you need to pass on information to other people as well. You rely on input from others, and they rely on input from you. Looking to the future, that necessity is not going to change.

Technology may modify the form of communication, but it will not eliminate the need.

Whatever you do to earn a living, you will find that getting advancements and promotions will require you to effectively communicate in the language of your profession; both orally and in writing. Communication skills are extremely important in professions such as medicine, the law, finance, and engineering. Would you want a doctor to tell you he maybe thinks he probably needs to, like, remove your thingamajig from your, like, whatchamacallit? How about a tax accountant who tells you he can't understand the tax codes because they're too hard to read and just too complicated?

I used to use an expression to sum up a statement without realizing that people I worked with were sick and tired of hearing me use it over and over again. Fortunately, one of my colleagues was considerate enough to tell me just how irritating my constant use of the phrase "and all that jazz" was to many of the people I was trying to communicate with. In this case, my choice of words had a negative effect on my ability to effectively communicate with my coworkers. This also illustrates the importance of listening as part of the communication process. I listened to my colleague and I acted on his input. Listening has been, and to some degree still is, one of my communication weaknesses.

Another communication problem I had to deal with – and that I'm still working on – was my tendency to interrupt other people when they were talking. I had the urge to jump in because I got excited about the subject and because I've always been quite opinionated. Aviation has a term for this. It's called "stepping" on someone. The term is used when one pilot is talking on the radio and another pilot breaks in and drowns out the first pilot. If I "step" on someone, neither party is heard well.

One area of communication that most of us frequently overlook concerns ourselves. We need to spend time communicating with ourselves. We need to constantly remind ourselves of our goals and how we plan to achieve them. Who better than ourselves to do that? Part of that internal communication should be focused on our general well-being that we can achieve through activities like meditation and mental self-examination.

Also, please be advised that how you communicate is not just about the words you use to express yourself or your command of the spoken language. It is about the composite picture you draw of yourself for others to observe. You communicate with a myriad of signals that can be both tangible and intangible. For example, your demeanor when you deal with people can be very revealing. Are you considerate toward all people or do you ignore some of them? Are you thoughtful to others? When someone is talking to you, do you look at the person or at something else? Do you show anger? Is your behavior sometimes influenced by a perceived need for attention or a craving for recognition? Are you assertive? Do you need to be heard? All of these traits are forms of communication.

A male conductor of an orchestra can appear to be professional by wearing a tuxedo and sporting a hairdo reminiscent of Albert Einstein; or an artist, actress or movie producer can wear outrageous clothing. However, many people in other professions would frown on a colleague who presented such an appearance. Like it or not, people have norms of acceptable behavior and appearance for their workplaces.

When I was involved with potential acquisitions, I liked to sit in front of the facilities being considered and observe the people who were entering and leaving. That gave me a feel for the nature of the operation inside. In some businesses, everyone was smartly dressed and presented a very polished appearance, while the people at other companies were much more casual. At some firms everyone seemed to be full of energy and excitement, while people appeared to be dull and slow-moving at others. All of those businesses, because of the people's actions, were communicating a great deal about their values. It was not difficult to understand what they were saying.

When you are in school you are communicating every day with your teachers as well as with your peers. What do you suppose you're telling them? Is your message the one you really want them to receive? Are you sending out conflicting or, perhaps, even false signals? Can you conclude that you are effectively communicating the right message to other people?

Remember, I'm not suggesting that you invent some ideal person who you imagine you are, but that you communicate who you really are to others. No one else can be you, nor can you be someone else. On the other hand, I'm not saying you can't improve who you are or set goals to communicate more effectively with others, because that is often exactly what you need to do. A major part of communication is constantly striving to learn from other people, to hear and understand what they are saying and doing, to observe those around you, and to absorb the world of stimulating activities in your everyday life.

It is of the utmost importance that you be properly understood. Understand?

About Leadership
You can be an effective leader

There is a chance that some of you will have an opportunity to be a leader, a person who others are expected to follow. Leadership frequently brings with it responsibilities at several levels, and at some point it should require accountability. To provide good and proper leadership, it is imperative that you use a finely tuned moral compass as a guide. You owe it to those who are trusting in you for direction.

I have read many books about business and business practices, and I can tell you that few of them offer easy, real-world, workable formulas for effective leadership. And it really serves no purpose to lead if your leadership is not effective. The biggest single factor is probably your own self-confidence.

How we lead is often an important factor in determining if we will be effective leaders and the kinds of people who will choose us to follow. I use the word "choose" on purpose; for it is up to those who follow to choose who it is they will allow to be their leader. Many people assume leadership positions but do not provide proper leadership on any level. And although there are situations where people may conclude they have no choice but to follow such a leader, as soon as they have an out they will take it.

Initially, people will usually follow any appointed leader. Even then, however, some do so halfheartedly. There are numerous reasons why this happens. It could be a difference in ages or an uninspiring leader. It might be a feeling of being led in the wrong direction or being assigned to a worthless task. It could be values that are not shared, bad communications, bad attitudes or, even worse, a lack of trust in the leader. It could be a damaged ego because someone didn't get the leadership position. Or maybe someone needs the job and is merely hanging on until something better comes along.

It is also critically important, when you are leading people, that the activity has a meaningful purpose. As my old friend Peter Drucker loved to point out: "There is nothing as useless as doing with great efficiency something that need not be done at all."

When I was president of the Kysor Industrial Corporation, I attended a meeting with some executives from the Ford Motor Company because Kysor supplied some of the parts for Ford trucks. During a conversation about the constant need to improve quality, one of the Ford executives told me about an experience he had with a Japanese company that Ford had partnered with.

As part of Ford's initiative to apply the same quality control measures to its administrative functions that it had successfully applied to manufacturing, Ford attempted to improve its accounts payable procedures by streamlining the workflow and reducing bottlenecks. When it started this effort, Ford employed about twenty-six hundred people in Accounts Payable. After several months of identifying problems and implementing improvements, Ford reduced that number to about eighteen hundred.

Ford was quite proud of how efficient it had become. Then one of the senior executives asked how Ford's results compared with other companies. So Ford asked its Japanese partner how many people they employed in Accounts Payable. The initial answer was eight. Ford, however, figured the Japanese had not understood the question. So it was rephrased and asked again, this time explaining that Ford's Accounts Payable Department included people who checked and counted the incoming parts and compared them to the invoices provided by the suppliers. Once verified and approved, the Accounts Payable Department would pay the vendors.

The Japanese responded to the rephrased question a few weeks later. Again, the answer was eight. When pressed on how they had accomplished all of that work with just eight people, the Japanese explained that they simply provided all of their vendors with a copy of the manufacturing schedule so the vendors would know what cars were being assembled each day. The vendors delivered the parts in time to be incorporated into the cars as needed. Since the Japanese company never shipped any cars with two steering wheels or without windshields or tires, they just counted the cars made each day and paid their vendors for the parts that each had supplied. They did not even try to do many of the things that Ford had accepted as being essential to the process. In short, Ford had found a way to do with greater efficiency many things that did not need to be done at all. For many years, Ford had simply been doing business as usual without ever questioning why.

I suspect that most people, deep down, prefer to follow. It is so much easier and less stressful to follow than to lead. But I assure you there is nothing more satisfying than leading people to successfully accomplish a worthwhile task.

In most companies, when people are promoted to leadership positions they are simply given the accoutrements of office – the desk, telephones, fancy new business cards, and name on the door. Whatever training they receive, if any, is focused on the product or procedures and not on the people who are being led. It is not unusual for a person to assume a job with no more than a cursory idea of what the job really is. You may find yourself in such a situation someday.

If you do, spend some time seeking advice from those around you. It is not a sign of weakness but of strength. Ask them what they think is the most important activity or function of your new job. Ask them what kind of help they think your area of responsibility can provide for them, how you can support them, and how they can support you. Listen to everyone and weigh the inputs. But in the end do what you feel is the right thing. Above all, pay attention to your own vibes.

In addition, do not lose your self-confidence and sense of worth or behave in a way that is not you. I'm not saying that you won't have self-doubts, but if and when you do, keep them to yourself and well hidden from your subordinates. No one wants to follow a leader who is not sure of himself or about what he is doing. But understand that self-doubt can be healthy if it causes you to do some introspective thinking.

Another thing to avoid is the feeling of self-importance that sometimes overcomes people when they assume a leadership position. Those who follow you, as well as your peers, will be quick to detect any such feelings. One good rule is to never take yourself too seriously.

Sometimes there is confusion about the role of a leader. It is not uncommon for people to assume that the leader is the most knowledgeable person in the group. That, however, is often not the case at all. For example, an engineer may be the best and the brightest when he assumes a leadership position, but after three years his knowledge may be outdated because he has not been able to keep up with the advances in his profession. He has devoted most of his time to managing his group, reviewing performances, assigning work, setting goals, and responding to requests for information about the group's activities. He is still the leader, but he is more like an orchestra conductor. His job is to get everyone to play together, not to be the best trumpet or cello player.

I tend to classify people who are in leadership positions into three broad categories: leaders, managers, and trustees. Leaders to me are the visionaries, the ones who see opportunities that few others seem to notice; people like Elon Musk at Space-X or the late Steve Jobs at Apple. Managers make sure the policies and procedures are followed. They are found in all large organizations and seem to exist disproportionately in government. They often say they would like to help, but it's against the company's policy or rules. Trustees are focused on preservation. They are very conservative, hate change, and are careful to avoid all risks. It is their job to make sure that no assets are ever squandered. All of these types of leaders can be invaluable in the right situation.

Companies frequently seem to grow more rapidly under people identified as leaders, and leaders seem to be attracted to industries with greater growth opportunities. They are often described as driven people with strong wills, impatient, and demanding. Manager-type personalities tend to wind up as leaders of less dynamic businesses and are focused frequently on cost controls. Their businesses tend to grow slowly. Trustees lead businesses that experience little or no growth, but they are intimate with every detail of their business. Another distinction is that real leaders generally tend to focus on external opportunities, while managers focus as much on internal matters as on external opportunities, whereas trustees are almost exclusively concerned with internal matters.

Middle managers are just that. They are not expected to provide a great deal of leadership except to keep their areas of responsibility in line with the organization's objectives. Like the captains of ships in a convoy, they maintain speed, direct their crews, and do no harm to the other vessels.

I once worked for a man who, whenever he was promoted to a new position, would take a quick look at the people who reported to him and randomly select someone whom he would fire on the spot. Later, when I became his peer, he told me he did that because he felt he didn't have time to earn the respect of his people and that the fear of being fired would make everyone work extra diligently. Not surprisingly, he too ended up getting fired.

When you become a leader at any level, be sure to concentrate on the mission of your area of responsibility. Don't worry about your next promotion. In the final analysis, proof is in performance. Be honest in your approach to people and tasks. Be sure you understand yourself, what your strengths and weaknesses are, and then try to place people around you who can complement your weaknesses or, better yet, build on your strengths. In other words, hire good people who can make you look good.

Be especially realistic about setting expectations. Everyone wants to please the boss, so it is common for subordinates to tell management they can complete a task in an unrealistically short time because that's what the boss wants to hear. You want to commit your team to a job with a challenging timeframe to show everyone you are a good leader. This can trap you into being a poor performer because deadlines will be missed and the boss will think it is your fault. It is your fault because you did not have the foresight to set a realistic goal.

One rule that worked for me in the long run was to under-promise and over-deliver. By that I mean I would fight for a realistic schedule for a given task and then beat it! I would determine what I believed was an appropriate time for my team to perform a task. Then I would build in additional time for unexpected events, because there always are some. Then, for a particularly difficult assignment, I would add a little more time as a safety measure. Some people think of this as "sandbagging," but I call it managing expectations.

At first it was hard to follow this procedure because upper management usually wanted things done sooner than I had estimated, and some of my subordinates would predict that the task could probably be done as quickly as the boss hoped. But I found that if I stuck by my guns I could, reluctantly perhaps, get a realistic time for my team to complete the project. Then I would challenge my team to beat the deadline and do a first-rate job.

Bosses are not dumb. They quickly figured out what I was doing. However, they also knew they could count on the job being accomplished, usually before the deadline, thereby giving them some time to make any necessary adjustments. The teams I led were not constantly hounded or held under the gun for missing deadlines and leaving management with no real idea of when the task would be finished. The aggravation I felt up front was considerably less than the consternation I would have experienced had the project been finished late.

Another thing you need to understand about leadership is that you have an obligation to educate your leaders about what you do and how to best measure your performance. I know this sounds strange, but you should not expect your boss to be intimately familiar with your daily routine. Your boss has other issues to deal with, and you are there to perform some of the tasks for which he is accountable. If your boss could do your job as well as everything else, he wouldn't need you!

If you closely examine a corporation and the duties and responsibilities of its people, you will understand that the ultimate responsibility for everything rests with the individual at the very top. It is true for just about every organization. Think of the people who start businesses. At first they do everything themselves. Then, as they find they have too much to do they either hire other people or purchase a service to do some of the things they were doing. But it is still the responsibility of the people who own the businesses to ensure they are run properly.

As an enterprise grows, it develops leadership positions such as a president, vice presidents, directors, and managers. Even though the person at the top has the global perspective, as well as the fiduciary responsibilities, for the business and is technically responsible for everything and everyone concerned with the enterprise, the people working for the person at the top may think they know more than he or she about what is best for the business. Some may even resent being told what to do. They want to decide for themselves what the job is. Despite those feelings, over time the organization will assume the personality of the person at the top because, as I mentioned earlier, subordinates learn what is important to the boss and respond to his or her desires. It is a continuous feedback loop. As people see how other people are rewarded, they will tend to emulate that behavior because they too covet similar recognition.

Every good leader is a good communicator. Communication is accomplished in many ways. There is, of course, the verbal and written word. There are also body language, demeanor, appearance, and actions. Believe me, if you are the boss, your every move is watched. It is what you do that counts, just as much as what you say. A leader is always communicating, whether intentionally or not. A leader has no casual moments.

Leaders are always on duty. There is truth to the saying that being the company president is the loneliest job in the world. Having been there, I learned that just about every person you deal with, in or out of the office, has an agenda. Everyone wants something from you. You learn that there are few people you can truly relax with and just about no one outside of your family from whom you can seek honest counsel.

Leaders at every level set the tone with all that they do and say. They come in all stripes, sophisticated or crude, smart or clever, arrogant or humble, wealthy or poor, well-dressed or sloppy, analytical or free spirited, and all the gradients in between. People at the top set the tone, and the longer they are there the more the organization reflects their personalities and values.

Be alert to the fact that, in a way, you become what you are. By this I mean that most people who are given leadership roles have already been identified as leaders by their behavior and demeanor. There is also truth in the old saying: "Dress for success." Dress is often an essential part of creating an aura of authority or accomplishment. In the entertainment industry, dress may be more essential than talent in some arenas. It is a business that requires the individual entertainer to attract attention while standing among an army of like-minded individuals. Only the most bizarre and outrageously looking or acting people can gain the notoriety needed to succeed in a big way. It's what draws us to watch them, and to be watched is to make money in the entertainment business.

After I was transferred from the Raytheon Missile System Division to the company's corporate office, I had the good fortune to work for Bill Pultz. He was nearing retirement and chose to mentor me in all things necessary for fitting into the corporate environment. He was one of the most ethical and principled men I had ever met. He was definitely everything you could imagine in an officer and a gentleman. He had graduated from Cornell, become a captain in the U.S. Army, a middle manager with General Electric, and had spent twenty years in the upper echelons of the Raytheon corporate office. Bill knew that, because of what he called my "humble origins," I had never been exposed to anything like the professional environment in which I found myself, and he wanted me to do well. He explained the importance of appropriate appearance including proper bearing, dress and grooming. Bill advised me about the proper shoes to wear (Johnson & Murphy), and how the laces should be tied. What I learned from Bill Pultz about bearing and appearance guided me during my entire career, including up to and into the board room.

Throughout history, dress, appearance, and bearing have conveyed authority. You can readily observe this, even at a local level, when a police or fire chief wears four stars, like those of a general, on his collar, or when a clergyman wears elaborate vestments trimmed in gold thread, or when a businessperson wears conservative and custom-fitted dark suits.

People are influenced by what they observe. I learned many years ago that the best place to go when I needed to use a restroom while traveling was not a gas station but the most upscale hotel in town. Walk in, and if you can't quickly find the restroom, ask at the desk. If you look important and if you convey confidence, most people will assume that you are important and treat you accordingly. That is why people go to such great lengths to wear the trappings of their office or position. Perception is reality! Your dress is part of the way you communicate to the world who you want them to believe you are.

Like so many others, I admired Mother Teresa. Just think of this small, fragile woman clad in her simple Indian sari caring for the poor of Calcutta. Compare that image to one of the pope attending Easter services in his splendid papal vestments. Who better conveys moral authority?

About Love

God gave you an infinite supply of love; please spread it around

Love is one of the strangest forces in the universe. We are all born with it. In fact, we are born with an infinite supply of it. It is up to each of us to decide how much of that infinite supply we use.

Hate, by the way, is not the opposite of love. It is merely the absence of love. Love is a force that unites as well as divides. It can overwhelm our senses, or it can enhance them and bring about a new awareness. While love is common to all of us, it is also true that some of us seem to be more susceptible to love's emotions.

We are seen as being loving because of our sensitivity to other people and their needs. How often do you meet someone who is unhappy with their life and everything around them? You know, the complainers, the ones who are never happy with anyone or anything. They lead miserable lives. It is sad, and I always feel bad for them because they have never learned how to embrace love. They have never learned to get up every day and enjoy themselves. They have never learned to feel the warmth and love that happy people share. I suspect, by the way, that many of these people behave the way they do because they live in fear of being rejected.

When you love the world and the people in it, the world and the people will love you back. So whether or not you will be loved is your decision. You choose the kind of day you will have every day, usually as soon as you awake up. If you tell yourself it will be another great day, it will be because your attitude is positive and you will look beyond any problems you might encounter. If you decide you are *not* going to love the world and the people you come across during the day, you will experience another miserable day on the planet.

It would not surprise to me to discover, when this life is over, that God chooses those of us who will share a heavenly afterlife based on how much of our infinite love we have spread around to humanity during our lives.

To love in a world that places a higher value on other virtues is not always easy. And there are so many types of love based on what, one might argue, are artificial premises. For example, people love their country, yet the boundaries of every country in the world have been established, directly or indirectly, by a superior force of arms or intimidation. Those with the most spears, guns, bombs, and rockets win. Realistically, then, countries are an artificial creation of someone's political will and military might.

Oddly enough, whether a country was on the winning or losing side when its geographic borders were established, its citizens are patriotic and passionate about their country. They love it! Unfortunately, there are those who love their country as it once was or what it might have been in terms of geography and refuse to accept political reality. This is especially true about countries that were once the heart of an empire. For example, some people in Greece never want that country to be reconciled with Turkey because they consider the western part of modern day Turkey to still be Greek territory, which it once was. Of course you have to ignore the fact that Greece was first consolidated by war and conquered by the Macedonians. Cypress, Serbia, Israel, Korea, Russia, Ireland and China are other examples of countries where significant parts of the populations are wrestling with identity problems.

Another impediment to love is bigotry. We observe it far too often in our daily lives because it rarely strays very far from the surface of human emotion. Bigotry is especially damaging when exploited by politicians who prey on citizens by taking advantage of their ignorance and fear. It takes long periods of acting in good faith to build trust among different people. But false rumors and clever innuendoes can unleash powerful negative forces. Political campaigns today are based almost entirely on creating false images of opponents, exploiting bogus issues, and avoiding real discussions about policies. The role of responsible voters is made more difficult with each election as political parties and candidates deliberately obscure the issues and generate more confusion. And everyone, it seems, is trying to rewrite history to suit their biases and ambitions.

Our society loves money, and we especially love people who are wealthy. Some of the moneyed people are admirable in their behavior, respectful of their fellow man, and known for treating people with the dignity that everyone deserves. On the whole, however, very few of us seem to be concerned with people's values if they have a lot of money. We're not nearly as concerned about how they acquired their wealth so long as they have it. Because of their wealth, those people are afforded status and privileges as if they were royalty. But they may not be any smarter or wiser or more loving than anyone else. Therefore, I urge you, don't judge people by the gold standard.

Be a champion to all people and strive to support the equality of mankind. Do not be afraid to love someone. Do not be afraid to love everyone! Care deeply about the people in your life, including yourself. If you can't love and care for yourself, how on earth are you going to care for others. While we are on the subject, let me mention how much it means to others, to older people in particular, to receive a kind word or deed from someone, especially from someone they love. A note or a phone call that says you are thinking of them and just want to say "hi" can mean more than you can imagine.

Please understand that extending yourself and being loving toward others does not mean that you permit them to walk all over you, take advantage of you, or be abusive toward you. It often means quite the opposite – that you feel it is necessary to demand changes in attitude or action from those you love. Being a loving person does not rule out the possibility of being a tough-minded individual. There are times when being hard on another person is appropriate because you are driven by your desire to help someone you love avoid a disaster that you believe could be a consequence of his or her behavior. Being firm with someone is not an encumbrance to being a warm and loving person.

A major obstacle to being the warm, loving person that you would like to be is the difficulty in understanding your expectations of how other people should relate to you. It is not always easy to accept other people as they are, and it is nearly impossible to understand why people sometimes behave the way they do. But accepting people for who they are is vitally important if you are going to show them love.

Open your mind and resist the temptation to prejudge others. Above all, be inquisitive about the people you meet. Try to understand how other people see things and what motivates them to say and act as they do. If you are judgmental of others, it will cloud your view of the world unless you can train your mind to look through those clouds and see the real people those clouds so often conceal.

About Marriage
A joint venture based on compromise and sharing

When you embark on a marriage, you enter into a relationship that has a considerably greater effect than merely separating you from "I" and forever joining you to "we." You cross a threshold into a relationship that impacts your emotional, economic, and personal well-being for the rest on your life. It is a threshold that, once crossed, can never be crossed back. There are only three options open to you after you have gotten married; you remain married, you are divorced, or you are separated by death. In any event, your life will never be what it was prior to committing to marriage.

Marriage, therefore, is something one should not enter into cavalierly!

Obviously, having been married for over fifty years, I believe in the idea of marriage. I define marriage as a commitment that two people make to each other, and I don't have any particular concerns about who the two people are in terms of sexual orientations, gender or race. It's their mutual love, understanding and commitment to each other that matters to me. Now, having said that, here are some thoughts I hope you will consider.

First and foremost, you should understand up front that you are dealing with something that will significantly determine how you spend the rest of your life. Marriage can be a rocket booster that takes you to places you never knew existed. Or it can become a horrific downhill ride to disaster. Or it can be any number of things in between. Often it's a rollercoaster ride – uphill and down, fast and slow. After all, it is a relationship with someone else, and we are all different. What determines much of the marriage experience is simply how different!

In your social circles are people you can easily relate to and who you enjoy being around. When you can decide whom to spend your time with, it's only natural that you choose to be with people you know, especially the ones you like and share common interests. There are times when you will be strongly attracted to a person, and the relationship becomes so special that you want to spend as much time as you can with that individual because you feel engaged and stimulated by being in his or her presence. Because you enjoy that person so much, you want to make them happy so they will want to be with you.

Now, however, it gets complicated!

As the two of you spend more and more time together, your body chemistry comes into play. Your hormones start raging, and before you know it, the topic is sex and you're making plans for that trip down the aisle. It all happens so quickly and easily.

But wait! There's more!

Now you've got to live together. And guess what? Those hormones begin to take vacations now and then, and all those quirky little habits that you once thought were so cute, or that you chose to ignore, are now becoming a bit annoying.

What happened? During all of the time you were enjoying each other's company and trying to impress one another, you were modifying your own behavior to ingratiate yourself with your beloved at the same time he or she was modifying his or her behavior to try to please you. You were both putting your best foot forward. Now you're married and the sense of urgency to please the other party has diminished somewhat. Welcome to the real world!

Now what do you do?

Chances are you will both want to try to work out your issues. After all, you both realize that you had such a strong bond in the beginning, and, being rational people, you will try to renew it. It will mean that both parties have to make some compromises, talk things out, and work things through. The degree of difficulty involved in this exercise will depend on several factors, many of which may well have had their genesis before your wedding. But the biggest determining factor by far is attitude.

Usually, when you are young you are full of optimism and prone to minimize the seriousness of the difficulties you encounter. That is an advantage in many ways because if you knew how difficult some things were actually going to be, you would never undertake them in the first place, and you might never know what you can resolve or achieve. When contemplating marriage, however, that optimism can cause you to develop unrealistic expectations about what life will be like with your new "partner". And the right word is partner!

The concept of marriage between two individuals who are in love is, historically, relatively new. Throughout most of civilization, polygamy and marriages of convenience have been the more common practices, and in some places they still are. People don't have to be in love, or even know one another, to get married. By the time I was a young man, however, a marriage between two loving people was considered a sacred bond that was not easily broken. But times and social mores have changed. We now live in a society in which marriage is not the most stable of relationships primarily because people feel they are not obligated to continue living in an unhappy union. Whatever its evolution, marriage works best if it is entered with a serious, long-term commitment as well as an appreciation of the value of stability and sacrifice.

When you enter into marriage, you are relinquishing sole ownership of your life and transitioning to a joint venture between yourself and your chosen partner. To develop a lasting partnership, that acceptance of change must be reciprocal. Both partners have to resolve to improve their lifelong commitment to each other.

Your grandmother and I have had to deal with many issues during our marriage, but we have always accepted the idea that what affects one of us affects the other. We took our commitment to each other quite seriously and felt it was our duty to offer support and encouragement to each other when it was needed.

We were both high school graduates working in low-level clerical jobs when we were married. We rented a small apartment on Rollstone Street in Fitchburg, and Nonna left her job to become a full-time mother just before Diane was born. We had already made our first big mistake. We each had medical insurance through our employers, but we had neglected to inform the insurance carriers of our marriage. Furthermore, insurance companies at that time did not cover births until nine months after a marriage was reported. Therefore, when Diane was born our insurance covered us only as individuals, not as a married couple. We had to pay all of the hospital and doctor bills for our new baby ourselves. We were already strapped financially, and that development only exacerbated our situation. Our doctor, however, delayed charging us and then asked for considerably less than he normally charged and allowed us to make monthly payments.

It was a difficult existence for us, one that we really did not want to continue living forever. Together we became convinced that the way out of our unfortunate situation was for me to find a better paying job. That could only occur by getting an education. So, essentially still newlyweds, we settled into a grinding routine designed to improve our economic well-being over the long run. Even though we were struggling to maintain our subsistence existence, we intentionally embarked on a course that would strain our resources even further. It was a risky strategy with considerable stress and strain built in.

The costs of going to Clark University absorbed fully half of my income for five years. Then I went to Suffolk University Law School, which depleted my income for another four years. We had nine years of deliberate sacrifice and hardship. And please understand that we had to deal with considerably more than economic strain during that time. It was a continuous sacrifice by both of us as we struggled to persevere day after day, week after week, and month after month with little relief from the demands on us; Nonna, without transportation, practically a prisoner at home while I was working by day and attending classes at night and stealing time to study. The highlight for us was the Sundays when we visited our parents, ate their food, and watched our children play with their cousins.

In the end, all those years of sacrifice paid off handsomely for the both of us. In fact, after I received my undergraduate degree from Clark, I secured a supervisory position in accounting at the Raytheon Missile Systems Division's plant in Andover, and that launched my professional career. After a few more years, my income was sufficient to provide Nonna with a car and some spending money and we were even able to muster the resources for her to travel with me on business trips.

Those nine years that I attended Clark and Suffolk universities, although strained and stressful, were happy years for us, and we have fond memories of the sacrifices we made and how they strengthened our bond as we dealt with the forces of the everyday world. It was far from fun and games and there were times when one or the other of us was nearly overwhelmed by the pressures. But we supported each other through it all and persevered. We now share a great sense of pride in our mutual accomplishment.

That experience was a blessing for us because we had to resolve our issues in ways that satisfied the both of us. We learned how to communicate with each other at an instinctive level. Let me tell you the down side of that, however. Some time ago, I was musing about something, and Nonna told me I shouldn't think like that. "What are you talking about?" I asked. "You don't know what I was thinking." To which she told me exactly what I was thinking. Now that's scary!

Some years ago, I listened to a radio interview with a doctor who had come to the United States from India, originally to attend Harvard Medical School. She was practicing medicine in Boston. She told the interviewer that she had been married for many years and had, I think, three children. What struck me was her explanation that she had not met her husband until her wedding day because her father had arranged her marriage. She strongly defended the practice and explained she was quite happy and had a successful marriage. She explained that many of her colleagues who had met their spouses on their own were unhappy in their relationships, and some were divorced, a fact she attributed to the American dating and engagement process.

Her father, the doctor believed, knew her well, maybe even better than she knew herself, and he had carefully selected a man he believed would be compatible with her. She argued, furthermore, that in America people marry someone they fantasize is perfect and then become disappointed when that person is not Prince Charming and isn't quite as flawless as imagined. Since most people have difficulty changing who they really are, one party eventually decides they can do better on their own and files for divorce. However, she argued, when two people who don't know each other are united in an arranged marriage, they both understand right from the start that they will have to put forth the extra effort to make their relationship work. They know they have to extend themselves to find happiness together. It means that both parties understand they will have to compromise and make sacrifices. Therefore, they each work at building a lasting relationship. I thought the doctor made some excellent points. It turns out that even in America the divorce rate is lower than normal for those in such arranged marriages.

I do not in any way want to discourage you from getting married. But I do want to alert you to some things that, in the course of your lifetime, can improve your odds for marital success.

One thing you should consider is your own lifestyle and the places you frequent, because you will probably meet that special someone during the ordinary course of living. If you spend your time at horse ranches, you just might meet someone who is into horses. So it follows that you can improve your chances of meeting someone with whom you can forge a lasting relationship if you travel in circles where people have interests similar to your own. The more you can narrow the differences and expand the common ground, the better off you'll be. For example, it is easier to find common ground if you have the same religious beliefs, similar ideas about recreation, work ethics, educational levels, cultural backgrounds and interests, senses of humor, values, and attitudes. By reducing the differences, you will reduce potential barriers to effective communication and understanding. It will be easier for you to share interests and enjoy each other's company.

It's also important to look for someone whose heart is in the right place. After all, marriage is about love.

Finally, remember that you and your tastes will change as you mature, especially after your twenties. What is important to you when you are twenty may not be as significant when you reach thirty. Ideally, your spouse will mature right along with you.

Graduating to Adulthood

There is so much to be gained and such great rewards in having the right partner. You are going to deal with so many issues in the years ahead, and it is much easier when you have a soul mate to share the good times, the load, the total experience. Being joined together by your children magnifies the rewards immensely. The love and happiness you will be privileged to share with your spouse for an entire lifetime is more precious than any other thing I can imagine. Being married has been the richest and most rewarding part of my life, and I sincerely hope all of you are blessed to share in a similar experience.

About Parenting

The most rewarding job in the world. Really!

When I think about the happy times in my life, I think about my children because they are the most frequent and constant sources of my enjoyment.

This is probably the most difficult subject for me to offer advice about simply because, in our situation, it was Nonna who bore the bulk of the parenting responsibilities. For the first years of our marriage, I was attending school every night after working all day. Then, after commuting from Fitchburg to my job at Raytheon in Andover for five years, and working long hours, I was promoted to a position in the Lexington corporate office that required extensive travel. That was followed by a move to Tyco International's corporate offices in Exeter, New Hampshire, with even more extensive travel requirements. At Tyco, I commuted to New Jersey every day. Then came two years of work in Phoenix, Arizona, and another twenty-seven months as finance director of Muirhead PLC English in Beckenham, England. I came home for a two- or three-day visit every second or third weekend.

Obviously, my schedule did not give me anywhere near as much time to be with my wife and children as I would have liked. I rationalized it as part of the price I had to pay to achieve the success that enabled me to provide my wife and children with the lifestyle I wanted them to have. In retrospect, it is one of the few aspects of my life I might do differently if I had the chance. I would seriously consider sacrificing some of my success for more time with my family.

During all those years, I truly relished all of my time with my family. I made every effort to spend what has become known as "quality time" with my children, and it wasn't because I was merely trying to do my job as their father. I derived a great deal of pleasure from being with them.

Despite my limited role in raising our children, I did spend enough time with them to learn some important things about parenting.

I discovered that children are the most interesting and entertaining people you will ever know. They enrich your life in ways that are absolutely incredible. They truly are one of life's great rewards!

Children adapt to their environment, and they need discipline to establish guidelines of proper behavior. Every family needs a disciplinarian as well as someone to provide unselfish love and devotion. Nonna was the disciplinarian in our household that she also filled with love.

Children observe and absorb what they see, hear and experience around them, and I'm sure your children will do the same. We all learn how animals and other living things adapt to their environments, but none adapt more quickly or completely than human beings beginning with their childhood years. They quickly learn, for example, that if mom says "no," they can ask dad who may say "yes." They can turn heartfelt tears on and off like a faucet or charm a grandparent into doing what they want with an innocent smile.

You will establish limits for your children in a number of areas either by intent or through default. You will quickly learn that the standards of behavior you expect of your children will absolutely need to be practiced by you if you expect them to be followed. Don't expect your children to say "please" and "thank you" if you don't. Your children learn from watching you! It is your example that counts. You set the standards. Perhaps the most important examples you will set have to do with values. Sometimes the rewards of parenting come from your children's comments. Mine have told me more than once that they remember times when a restaurant server or a store clerk gave me a bill that was incorrect in my favor. I would point out that the total was too small or that they had omitted an item they should have included on my bill. I voluntarily paid more money than I had to. But I had done the right thing and, more important, I had demonstrated by example an important value – honesty.

Life will be easier on you if you take the time to think through the consequences of your actions prior to undertaking them. It is so important that you fully appreciate the commitment you make when you put yourself in a position to become a parent. Yes, it is extremely rewarding. But it is also extremely demanding on you and your personal and financial resources. That child will be your responsibility for eighteen years by law and, probably, for longer than that. I recently read that the total average cost of raising a child from birth until the age of eighteen is $275,000. Private schools and expensive cars can significantly increase that amount. My point is that you will be making a major trade-off in your life, and that shouldn't surprise you. I will tell you this. There never seems to be a perfect time to have children. Nonna and I agree that all four of our children were the results of "accidents." We have no regrets. But if that average cost for raising each child is correct, our little family cost us a bit more than a million dollars. Now let's see. How many vacations is that? It doesn't matter. I wouldn't trade the experience for anything.

What I am trying to accomplish with this book is a good deal of what you will try to accomplish as a parent. You will need to teach your offspring the rules of life and how to deal with their fears and unexpected situations. You will certainly try to give them unconditional love and support and nurture them through their stages of physical, emotional, and intellectual growth and maturing. You will guide them as they set goals that lead to achievements they can take pride in. You will be the guardian of their health and well-being. You will influence their spiritual development. They will learn the norms of acceptable behavior with their siblings, other family members, and other people by observing how you interact with others. Your children will deal with their mistakes based on your examples: How you correct your bad decisions or how well you overcome setbacks and plot new courses of action. You will teach them about finances and set lasting examples by your spending habits and decisions about buying homes and replacing automobiles and appliances. Whatever you do, wherever you go, they will always be watching, absorbing and learning. You, therefore, have an incredible responsibility!

One major mistake I have observed far too frequently involves parents who try to be their children's best friends. Trust me, there will be ample opportunities to have relationships with your children that more closely resemble friendships when they have become adults. Until then, you are their adult parent and they are your children, and there is no escaping that symbiotic relationship. When parents try to be a "friend" to their children, they invariably pretend they are young and hip to the world and consequently fail to establish proper guidelines for their offspring. Both end up lacking discipline.

When your children grow to maturity, it is the values you instilled in them that will act as their North Star in life. Those learned values are the reference points they will continually use to distinguish between the right and wrong paths as they journey through their lives. They may sometimes regard those values as their conscience speaking to them, but it is the voice of you, their parents, whispering through their minds. Someday your children will hear your voice guiding them through a dilemma, and you want that voice to be one of great principle.

Please understand that every one of your children will be unique. True, they may not look alike, but they will differ in personalities and interests even more. Some children are perfectly comfortable playing by themselves, while others always want their friends around. Some have more vivid imaginations than others. Some are always cheerful and forgiving. Some are impatient and short-tempered. The list of differences is almost endless. The bottom line is that each child has different needs, and you can't assume that one of your children will in any way be similar to another. The experience of raising one baby will not be repeated when you raise a second one. My daughter Diane was docile and hardly ever made a fuss when she was young. We could easily take her when we visited other families because she was what we now call a low-maintenance child. Peter, our next born, was almost the complete opposite, always active and inquisitive. He needed constant attention. There was nothing wrong with his behavior. It was just that he had totally different needs and desires than his older sister, and we had to adjust to that reality.

Yes, there are burdens that go with raising children, and there will be times when you ask yourself if it is all worth it. But, in the end, you will be happy that you accepted the challenge. It is absolutely true that your children, and their children, will keep you young. Let me assure you that the rewards far outweigh the hardships.

About Lifestyle
You live the life you choose, so choose well

I want to pass on to you what I have learned about the importance of choosing the right lifestyle, about making good decisions for your life. This is not merely hearsay information or things I have read about. Rather, it is based on what I have experienced personally. I don't want you to lose track of what is important. I want you to focus on a good and valuable life versus, say, a "high" life.

How we choose to live our lives has an enormous impact on our health and general well-being. All of us are familiar with the harm that alcohol abuse or drug addiction can do to an individual's appearance. We also have some idea of what those habits can do to a person's ability to think clearly. That is because we have observed some of those unfortunate people firsthand and witnessed their sometimes-bizarre behavior. Many end up living on the street.

On the other hand, we see on television, in movies, and in the print media examples of nearly perfect looking individuals such as models, athletes and rock stars.

The rest of us live somewhere in between.

What I have found is that there is a direct connection between how we feel and how we behave. When we feel good, we are more energetic in what we do and in what we say. And while feeling good physically is very important, feeling good mentally is what really counts. To be effective, we need to be enthusiastic about our work and our relationships with others. People who are truly happy seem to radiate that feeling. I like to think of Mother Teresa. When she walked into a room filled with people, they could feel her presence, her warmth and joy. It truly radiated!

It is also evident when we are depressed and down. I have known many fellow employees during my career who constantly complained about their job, their boss, the company, or how unfairly they were being treated. Those people were clueless about why they didn't get promoted or why they received the smallest raises. It never occurred to them that their attitude was retarding their progress. Most of them suspected that it was politics or some grand conspiracies that held them back. They would often point out, for example, that they had more seniority than the people recently selected for better assignments.

Over time, I realized that the people who complained the most were also sick more often than their colleagues and frequently experienced other physical problems. How they lived and how they perceived their lives clearly influenced how they felt. Lifestyle and well-being are in fact married to each other.

From my experience, the most important thing we can do to ensure we have a positive attitude is to stay fit – physically and mentally. Regular exercise in some form is not an option. It is an absolute necessity.

Only through exercise can we stay agile. Again, I mean intellectually as well as physically agile. Agility is the key to our well-being. The definition of agile is "quick and well-coordinated: active; lively: mentally acute or aware; brisk, or spry". That is what you want to be and how you want others to see you.

I have been in good shape for most of my life. It was not because I followed any particular exercise program. Rather, I have always been a very active person by nature. When I was married, at twenty-one, I stood five feet ten and weighed 136 pounds, with a twenty-six inch waist. One of my early bosses told me I reminded him of a three-year-old child because some part of my body was always moving. Another boss said that he had never met anyone with as much energy as I had. He said he knew people who burned the candle at both ends but that I was the first person who also burned it in the middle!

I had a positive, can-do attitude, and I was genuinely happy even though I was never fully satisfied with my progress. I always thought I could do more than what I was doing and that I could do it better. I truly believe that I achieved much of my business success because people liked me. I was a nice guy.

My bosses enjoyed my company. They knew I was loyal; always trying hard and never taking myself too seriously. There were always people around me who were smarter than I was and certainly much more knowledgeable about what had to be done, but some of them were handicapped by their attitudes. Often they were just too smug about their knowledge or they were reluctant to share their know-how with others lest someone else get the credit.

I was always focused on how to best accomplish what needed to get done without regard for who got the credit. I figured that if I just kept my head down and did the job, the rewards would follow. Proof to me was always in the performance. And it worked!

When I moved from California to Michigan in 1990, I was in great shape both physically and mentally. I was fifty-two, weighed 168 pounds and was running about five miles every workday.

Living in northern Michigan made it extremely difficult to continue running. I was traveling much more frequently, and the winter weather made it challenging to run when I was at home. My exercise routine began to slip. Then it became nonexistent. I began gaining weight. I hit two hundred pounds and my waist stretched a thirty-eight inch belt. I was in a rut. I didn't seem to have enough energy to get through a day. More insidiously, I was losing my zest for life, my interest waned, and my attitude changed. I was not happy with myself, and it showed in my dealings with others. I had no one to blame but myself. I had to change. It was time to get hold of myself; to get back on track. The key was to start exercising again.

That was easier said than done, however, because even though I had jogged five miles a day for many years, I now struggled to run half a mile. So at sixty I resolved to start walking. It took a full year to comfortably walk three or four miles every morning. I started walking a mile and then walked longer distances as I got back into shape and started to feel better.

Now that I am in my seventies, I know it would take even longer to get fit if I stopped exercising again and slip into my former ways. That has become my incentive to keep walking. Meanwhile, my attitude has improved, and I know that in another year I will again weigh less than 170 pounds. That is my goal because I know that when I reach it I will feel absolutely great and have lots of energy. My doctor advised me to get down to 182 pounds. I've already done that!

Staying mentally agile requires the same kind of discipline. You need to develop a strong intellectual curiosity. It is amazing how interesting people, places, and things can be. Make it a point to learn about foreign countries and cultures even if you have not visited them. I exercise my brain by reading, doing crossword puzzles, and closely observing the world around me – the landscape, trees, and stars. It is important that I keep my life in balance. I have been greatly enriched by developing an eclectic variety of interests. My quest for diversity has kept me engaged in such interesting things as poetry, history, philosophy, law, science, cartoons, space, astronomy and cosmology, travel, language, aviation, theater, birds, music, art, gardening, museums, sports, anthropology, weapons, politics, business, adventure, and even fish. My life has been a great adventure because of all the different things I have done and continue to do and all of the interesting things I enjoy studying.

In the end, your lifestyle is about you – the things that interest you and the things you care about. Develop a genuine passion for your life and the people in it. Know that when you have passion you will have courage. With courage you will not hesitate to defend the things you believe in. Your passion, courage, and beliefs will identify who you are to the world. My advice, therefore, is that you open your mind to a great many possibilities and then focus on the kind of life you want to live.

Please don't forget to enjoy yourself along the way. Go to a baseball game or a Super Bowl. Experience the Olympics! Travel at every opportunity. Take in an opera and a symphony. Visit museums or other places that interest you. Walk in the woods, hike the hills, and visit lakes and the seashore. Absorb your surroundings and all of the wonderful people and things that add stimulation and excitement to your day. Make your life more interesting by sharing your experiences with the people you love, and they will profit from it as well.

About Goals

Know where you're going; what needs to be done. Then do it!

When I think about goals and priorities, the first thing that comes to mind is discipline. It requires an element of discipline to effectively establish goals, determine priorities, and to follow through with the actions necessary to reach your objectives. It can be a rigorous undertaking. If there is little or no discipline, then setting priorities becomes just another wasted exercise.

Procrastination is one of the most common of human conditions. We just can't seem to do what we want to do when we want to do it. Equally perplexing is our belief that being busy equates to accomplishment. That's not always the case. However, the people who accomplish things are the ones who do things. I know that seems like basic common sense. Nevertheless, very few of us are known as doers.

We make many excuses to ourselves and to others for putting off the tasks we are facing. They are commonly generated by our self-doubts or because we want to do or are doing other things. We also often forget that not making a decision is, in fact, making a decision. We play games with ourselves to justify our behavior. Whatever the cause, the result is always the same. We delay. We avoid. We excuse ourselves. And, whenever possible, we try to get someone else to do it.

I explained earlier why it is important to be healthy of mind and body; how I try to start each day by going for a walk outdoors or by going to a fitness club to walk or do some strength training. How many times do you think I get up in the morning and say to myself: "I really don't feel like walking today?" How many times do you think I have to drag myself out the door? It can be very tempting on cold, raw mornings to simply relax with a hot cup of coffee and the morning newspaper. I have tried, many times, to avoid exercising by telling myself that it's just one morning out of many and that I should reward myself once in a while by taking the day off.

I can't tell you how many times I have had to remind myself that just because I don't feel like doing something doesn't mean I shouldn't do it! You, too, have to remind yourself of the same thing. Bear in mind that when you condition yourself to follow through on what you have set out to accomplish, you have learned the key to self-discipline.

As an aside, one of the most valuable lessons you can learn in college is how to meet the deadlines for papers semester after semester. You learn how to complete a task in a certain time, and that discipline will serve you well throughout your career.

After you have mastered the concept of self-discipline, you can concentrate on your priorities, set your goals, and focus on the tasks that require your attention first. It's so much easier to get someplace if you have a good idea of where you're going.

"Control your future or someone else will." You will hear that expression more than once. It's another way of saying don't just float down the river of life. Please understand that there are few things as basic in life as the idea that you need to establish goals if you want to achieve results. Indeed, it is essential.

That doesn't mean you can't dream. It's OK, even a good idea, to dream. Just base your plans on those dreams and set your goals accordingly.

I was a big dreamer when I was in high school. So much so that other students would tease me about some of the things I told them I would do. For example, I told them I would become a millionaire. I told them I would fly faster than the speed of sound, as Chuck Yeager had done, and that someday I would go into space. I told them I would travel the world and stay in the best hotels and eat at the finest restaurants. I even told them that one day they would see my name in *The New York Times* and *The Wall Street Journal*.

My friends laughed at me because they knew where I came from. They knew I was one of the kids who were living in near-poverty, with little chance of going to college. To them, my declarations were idle boasts and pure fantasies. The truth is, they were fantasies to me as well. But it didn't mean they couldn't come true. For me, those fantasies were like a compass. They told me where I was going. I turned them into my long-range goals. In the end, I achieved all but one of them. So far I have not gone into space.

It is easy to focus on turning your dreams into reality because your dreams make you feel good, and working toward those dreams is always a worthwhile experience. It is essential that you know where you are going and that you chart your course toward that end. You need to start thinking about setting your long-range goals early in your life to give you plenty of time to make those dreams come true. And don't hold back on yourself. Be audacious! Take the time to write them down and get yourself pointed in the right direction. Understand that you will be able to make numerous mid-course corrections as you proceed. Start with big ideas but, at first, take small steps. Be patient and try not to get too far ahead of yourself. Also, don't confuse those goals with wealth-building. That is a separate objective that I will address in another chapter.

It is best to establish your long-range goals without hard and fast deadlines. That way you can set flexible deadlines for intermediate objectives. You need to concentrate on devising a written one-year plan with specific objectives. But set a time limit for completing each part of this plan. Someone once told me that a task without a time limit is not really a task. Then, review your goals on a regular basis and make any necessary course corrections. Place your written goals where you will see them, in a drawer for example, and whenever you open that drawer, look at what you promised yourself you would do that week. And don't wait until Friday to do it. Ask yourself what you will do that day to get you closer to achieving your goals. And understand that it's not all that easy to do so because we really have no idea what will happen tomorrow, never mind next week or next year.

If it turns out that a step you planned to take towards a goal is impossible because circumstances have changed, make an adjustment. As you work on your plan, you will become increasingly aware of information that will help you. That will happen because you will be alert to sources of information that you might not have previously paid attention to. Your antenna will be up. You will seek out and find people with a common interest who will help you. The Internet, of course, is a fantastic information tool. It has made it so easy to explore other people's ideas and information pertaining to your goals.

Telling the world what you are going to do is another way to help you achieve your goals. Believe me, it is not farfetched to say that my pride kept me focused many times after I had told others what I was going to do. I didn't want to have to admit I couldn't do it.

My friend Miguel was in his mid-twenties when I first met him in Sarasota, Florida. He is Spanish and had come to the United States to learn to fly because it was much less expensive than it was in Europe where general aviation facilities were not as accessible. In over a dozen years, I have watched him do much of what I described. He had decided just before I met him that he wanted to be a test pilot or an astronaut, goals that were considered outrageous when he set them. At the end of each year Miguel has faithfully worked out his plans for the next year. He undertook that annual exercise with great enthusiasm and has always been excited to share his revised plans with me. Sometimes it didn't seem that Miguel was making much progress, and some years were difficult. But he is now a certified test pilot and very close to achieving both of those goals. He is a great example of the value of making a plan and sticking to it. Just as I have done so many times already, once Miguel has reached a goal, he establishes new goals based on his dreams for the future.

No attribute is more important in achieving your goals than tenacity. It is just as important, if not more so, than intelligence. We can study and think forever, but it's what we do that counts. As former General Electric chairman Jack Welsh put it: "If you're going to talk the talk, you're going to have to walk the walk."

After you set your objective, never give up until you accomplish it or unless you become convinced that it will not lead where you want to go.

Graduating to Adulthood

Understand that lifetime careers and attaining goals generally follow a path that can be visualized like a pair of funnels with the two small ends facing each other.

When you are in high school looking forward, you have almost endless possibilities to contemplate. You are entering the funnel. Soon you are forced to discard many options as you narrow your focus and approach the small part of the funnel. You must decide whether to go to college or to find a full-time job. If you decide on college, which one? And what to study? Will it be accounting, mechanical engineering, history, pre-med, or pre-law? You may then go on to graduate school and become even more focused on a narrow, or specific, discipline. After you complete your formal education and enter the professional world, your options and opportunities will again begin to expand, and you will have many more choices to consider. Now you are exiting through the wide end of the other funnel into a richer, fulfilling life.

Not everyone has to set goals to become an astronaut or to be elected president of the United States. Goals can include writing a book, or landing the lead in an off-Broadway play, or learning French and then visiting Paris, or climbing Mount Everest or Mount Washington. Perhaps you want to pursue a business venture. Whatever you desire, it can only happen if you commit yourself to its accomplishment. The key to success always depends on actions. If you don't act, you won't get there.

Only you can determine what your expectations are. Only you can decide where you are going. Only you can make your dreams come true!

About Wealth
Pay yourself first and you will naturally accumulate wealth

What does wealth mean to you?
A big house or lots of toys!
Earning large paychecks!

Enjoying a lifestyle of travel or leisure!
Having financial freedom!

Happiness!

Enjoying intellectual freedom!

Living in good health!

Clearly it means different things to different people, but most of those ideas are, in the end, directly related to your monetary wealth. Properties and "stuff" are connected to money, of course, but travel, free time, and even better health are also favorably affected by your wealth. There is little doubt: Your wealth is an important element in the overall quality of your life.

So to the question: What is wealth?

Here is the dictionary definition: "A great quantity or store of money or property of value, a plentiful amount, and the state of being rich; prosperity, affluence, opulence, and fortune."

To me, however, wealth is simply having the financial freedom to enjoy a happy, satisfying, stress-free and worry-free life. Having enough to do what you like to do.

Doing so, I find, generally doesn't cost all that much money after all; which ultimately means the dollar amount of accumulated wealth may not be as much as might at first be imagined.

But please understand, if you learn nothing else, that any real financial wealth is accumulated through disciplined investing over an extended period of time.

The sooner you start, the better your chances. It requires a genuine commitment to honor a promise you have to make to yourself to maintain a lifetime of continued saving. It needs to be akin to a religious belief that you practice faithfully.

One source of confusion about wealth is easy to clarify. Wealth is not income. Just because you enjoy a good income does not mean you are wealthy. It simply means that you can pretend to live as if you are wealthy until you have less income. That could happen if you lose your job or get sick or have to take a leave of absence. True wealth means being able to live the life you desire without any income other than what is generated from your assets. You don't need a job to do the things you like to do. You may have a job, but it is because you enjoy working while you continue to build your wealth. About twenty-five hundred years ago, the great Chinese philosopher Confucius, said: "Choose a job you love, and you will never have to work a day in your life." It is one of the reasons why Confucius is still admired for his great wisdom.

The key to wealth building is easy to say but not always easy to accomplish: Pay yourself first!

How do you pay yourself? You essentially make it a hard and fast rule that you live by. Look, when you earn money you use it to pay your bills. You pay your rent, your electric bill, your phone bill, and your other expenses. What I am advocating is that the first person you should pay is you – before the landlord, the electric company, or the telephone company. The purpose for earning money should not be to simply pay everybody else and end up with nothing for you. You earned it! You need to accumulate money for your own sake and to eventually achieve independence, so it is critically important that you pay yourself first.

And do so with each and every paycheck. No exceptions and no excuses! Pretend that you are sixty years old with just five years to go before you retire. That will help you to focus as well as to develop a sense of urgency for your saving discipline. As you get busier with your life, you lose track of how quickly the days go by. The next thing you know, forty or fifty years have gone by whether you have saved or haven't saved, whether you were disciplined or not. You should also know that your ultimate financial success is not determined by your income but by your expenses.

It bears repeating: Your financial success will be determined by what you spend, not by what you earn.

I submit that everyone can live with less than they have and certainly with less than they earn. In my youth there were times when I lived for two days on a single box of Corn Flakes. On the other hand, most people feel they need to have more and that they also need to earn more.

The media bombards us with "buy now" advertising with the intent of convincing us that we should not wait to buy what we want. We are urged to treat ourselves now. We hear how easy it is to enjoy things today and pay for them later. The Internet is full of algorithms and filters that focus marketing efforts and advertising on our interests. We are told continuously that we work hard and, therefore, deserve to be rewarded now. Charge that cruise vacation or your trip to Disney World now! It's the American way. Don't deny yourself all those good times in life that are "priceless."

I'm sorry, but contrary to all those commercials, you don't deserve the so-called "good life" until you earn it! The equation clearly is earning it, then saving it, then spending it if needed. It is not spend, earn, and never save!

Understand that the disciplined saving I'm advocating is designed to create wealth. It is not for a "rainy day fund." You should set up a separate emergency fund for those truly unexpected expenses. No, it will not be easy, but everyone can do it! Be resolved. There is no valid reason for you not to do it. You really can achieve a worry-free life.

Ask yourself this question: "Are people from Belarus, Costa Rica, India, Brazil, Cambodia, Mexico, or Nigeria smarter than I am?"

I'm sure you don't think so. Then why is it that many of those people leave their countries, come to the United States, many unable to even speak English, and succeed in living the American dream while you just can't seem to get started?

Look around and you can observe how these people are so easily contrasted to your peers. If you watch your friends, and maybe yourself, you will see that most are struggling with a mountain of debt and are living the American nightmare instead of the American dream. How do you pay all the bills that you owe? The newly arrived seem to be satisfied by working in 7-Elevens, gas stations, motels, or the food-service industry, often for the minimum wage. They frequently have more than one job.

It may surprise you to learn that these people often have little or no debt, that many are sending money to their families in their countries of origin, and that they may be saving money for themselves or their children as well. Meanwhile, you and your friends are stressed out while going to college or working in professional environments, with bills to pay and no real savings.

The difference is mindset!

One big difference is a ready, almost enthusiastic willingness to "pay the price." The immigrants live on only what they need until they accumulate the hard cash to acquire what they want. That is often an education for their children. They are not hindered by pride or held back by concerns about what other people may think.

What they want is no different than what you already have, except they don't get it on credit. Immigrants really own what they have. They resist impulse buying and live a frugal lifestyle in order to reach a greater goal. If you find it nearly impossible to control your own spending, cut up those credit cards and only purchase items with the cash you have on hand.

One word of caution: You must always remember that you never buy anything that is not absolutely essential to your survival until you have paid yourself first.

When you've earned your money by working, you should have enough respect for yourself to keep a fair share of the reward. Discipline yourself to think in terms of what you need, not what you want. Start simply with a savings account. If you work where you can have part of your pay automatically transferred into your savings, sign up for it. You won't miss what you don't see, and it will help maintain the saving discipline.

Be sure to sign up for employer 401K and Roth IRA programs whenever possible. These programs are a great way to enhance your own wealth-building. Where else can you increase your money just by making a deposit? And it's tax deferred or, in the case of the Roth, tax free on withdrawal.

When you get the feeling that you are sacrificing too much in order to save, remind yourself that you only need what you need, nothing more. I'm sure you can recall an experience when you or your parents purchased something that you thought you absolutely had to have, only to find that as soon as you acquired it, it became much less desirable. Then, as sure as sunlight, there was something else that you knew you just had to have.

Think like Buddha and rid your mind of material desires.

You may never have realized that more than a million dollars will pass through your hands during your working years. It's a sobering thought!

Chances are you will actually earn, and spend, far more than a million dollars during your lifetime. If you work from the time you are twenty until you are seventy, you will have worked for fifty years. If your average earnings during that time are just twenty thousand dollars a year, you will have made one million dollars! Since you will earn far more than that on average, in all likelihood several million dollars will pass through your hands. Just as amazing is how hard it is to keep some of that money for yourself, but that is exactly your challenge!

I find it so very sad that many of the people I've known over the years, people who had good jobs and earned an average of $50,000 a year, some who earned $80,000, and many who earned more than $100,000 a year for twenty years or more, end up with nothing. They have little or no savings. They still have a mortgage. They still have car payments. Many are still paying off loans for their children's education. All those thousands of dollars, year in and year out, and they spent it all! In fact they spent even more! That's why they are still in debt!

I don't want you to ever find yourself in that situation. I don't want you to spend your whole life working and then have little or nothing to show for it. If you adopt the pay-yourself-first rule, you will accumulate the wealth you need to be independent when you reach retirement age. It may surprise you to learn that I have no pension, just Social Security. It's not a problem because I have a lifetime of savings to provide for our needs.

This is one area where you definitely need to be selfish. You need to provide for your own future. Frankly, it is also the best thing you can do for your children and maybe your grandchildren as well, because if you are independent and have provided for your needs, then no one else will be burdened with that responsibility. Please understand that you will be told by many people – including your bosses, stockbrokers, insurance representatives, and time-share, condo, and home-sales people – that they can help you make the right decisions. They will tell you in all kinds of ways that you would be making a wise choice if you just trust them. DON'T! They are motivated by a desire to divert some of the money that is passing through your hands into theirs. As a matter of fact, you may even find yourself employed by a company in which your success will be based on how well you can convince other people to trust you and purchase that company's products or services. But also understand that you can never effectively delegate to anyone else your responsibility to save an adequate amount or to properly provide for your future.

The United States is said to have a service economy. How do service industries provide their services? How do they prosper? Many, such as restaurants, plumbers, electricians, computer techs, and laundries, provide a tangible service that you can measure quite easily. Many other services are less tangible, and their values are harder to measure. For instance, what is a stock broker's or a real estate agent's advice worth to you? How do you evaluate options on insurance policies? How do you find the mortgage loan that best fits your needs? How do you decide what university you should attend or what career you should pursue? So many things require special knowledge, and since you can't master everything, you will depend on others to provide you with the information or service you seek.

As you gain experience with these experts, you will discover that some are very good and worth their weight in gold while others are completely incompetent or even dishonest. Most will fall somewhere in between. In essence, most people acting in an advisory capacity are narrowly competent. Why?

It takes hard work to maintain proficiency in a professional field. What tends to happen is that practitioners find they can get by with a limited knowledge of most of the options available in their field, but they acquire an in-depth knowledge of one product or service which they then try to apply to all their clients – whether it's appropriate or not. For example, in my experience with mortgage loan officers, most of the more successful ones possess an in-depth knowledge of one particular kind of mortgage loan offered by one investor. They find that the more they deal with the same kind of mortgage, the easier it is to process the loan through the labyrinth of red tape. The natural consequence being that the loan officer will steer the client into the one mortgage that is easiest for the loan officer to process. With this example, you can see why it is incumbent on you to at least become familiar with the different kinds of mortgage options that are available in the marketplace.

Think hard about what you want and why you want it. Then ask yourself whether you really need it. You will be surprised by how little you actually need.

Now think about your options:

Do nothing OR start saving....NOW

Keep spending OR cut your expenses....NOW

Increase your debt OR establish your savings discipline....NOW

Keep drifting OR take control....NOW

I have learned much of this information – but not all of it – on my own. To help you understand my message, I urge you to read an old book, *The Richest Man in Babylon* by George Samuel Clason. In it you will read about the lessons learned by a man named Arkad who seeks to learn the secret to wealth from the richest man in ancient Babylon. It is a short book. I strongly recommend that you read it soon and then read it again in a few years.

About Investments
It's all about long-term gain

What to do with all of the money you have accumulated by paying yourself first is always a pleasant dilemma to be faced with. It is an area that can be confusing or simple, depending on how you approach it. Confusing in the sense that there are numerous investment options offered by financial institutions, real estate firms, and insurance companies; and simple in that these options can be condensed into a few select categories and managed for you by fiduciaries, if necessary.

Your options are essentially savings accounts, real estate, the stock market, or owning your own business.

During periods of modest to rapid economic growth, almost all investments will show reasonable growth. There is a saying in economics that "a rising tide lifts all boats". Since long-term economic growth is in no way assured, the wise investor – that's you – will look for vehicles to safeguard assets during difficult economic times when the economy is stagnant or shrinking. Your objective should be to seek the maximum financial reward with minimal risk to your capital. Capital, by the way, is just a fancy word for money or money equivalents.

Probably the easiest investment vehicle to understand, other than a savings account, is real estate because of the tangible nature of property. You can see it and touch it. It is common knowledge that the market for single-family homes in a given area will rise and fall over time depending on the health of the local economy. Unlike the prices for gasoline, housing prices do not change on a daily basis. They usually change slowly over months or years, often rising or falling in low, single-digit percentages. Over time they seem to keep up with the increases resulting from inflation. Inflation occurs when something costs more in the future than it does today because of the decrease in the buying power of money in the market place. Be advised that you will experience inflation firsthand sooner or later because that is how the federal government will pay for its large deficits of the past forty years. The feds will pay off the deficits with dollars that are worth less than today's dollar is worth.

When the economy is doing well, realtors, mortgage bankers, and many financial managers will tout home ownership as an investment; the assumption being that home values will continue to rise over time and that if you purchase a house today and sell it in five, ten, or twenty years you will receive more money than you paid for it. On the surface, that seems to make sense. However, it is not quite that simple because home ownership has costs that are not reflected in such a basic purchase and sale-price analysis.

Most people who purchase a home acquire a mortgage from a bank for a substantial portion of the price, usually between eighty and ninety percent, that they pay to the seller. The same is true for investment properties. A mortgage requires the buyer to pay interest on the amount borrowed. In an average interest environment during a normal market, the final amount paid for the house could total as much as three times the original purchase price. In other words, you could end up paying the bank a total of $900,000, depending on the interest charges, for a house you purchased for $300,000.

Even in markets where interest rates are most favorable to consumers, the interest costs will about double the total amount of money paid out. In addition, mortgage interest is front-loaded. That means that your payments go almost entirely toward the interest during the early years, and it is not until several years later that you start paying off the principal. Therefore, after five or six years of home ownership, you will still owe the bank nearly the same amount you originally borrowed. That is one of the ways banks make money.

In addition to the mortgage interest, you will have to pay real estate taxes, purchase homeowners insurance, and cover maintenance costs. In the end, it is still only an educated guess about what the future market value will be. So, in the long run, the total amount of money you will have to pay for your home will be a multiple of the original price because of the interest, taxes, and other expenses. You can see from all of this that trying to determine whether purchasing a home can really be considered an investment is not as easy as it at first appears. That is why it is wise when you are young to resist the temptation to purchase a single-family home too soon, other than as a rental property that is strictly an investment. It may be your own ego that entices you to buy a house before you are really ready. You may desire the personal satisfaction of owning your own home, or you may want to be seen as successful in your community. Be patient. Before you make a commitment to purchase real estate that you plan to occupy yourself, take the time to thoroughly compare the total costs of homeownership with the expenses of renting. Don't forget to include in that analysis the amount you would have earned on your investments if you had not withdrawn the funds for the house.

Purchasing real estate for investment purposes, on the other hand, should be strictly a numbers game. You should be focused solely on the return you can earn on the money you plan to invest using your known expenses with reasonable contingencies added in. And don't forget to compare your real estate investment opportunity with other investment options.

If you do become interested in real estate for investment purposes, there are basic formulas readily available to help you evaluate the financial aspects of any transaction. These formulas are not complicated and are easily found in almost every real estate investment guide. One such guide I recommend is *The Millionaire Real Estate Investor* by Gary Keller. It contains excellent guidelines and worksheets to assist you in evaluating potential investment properties and determining their relative worth.

One big advantage in property investments is the availability of financing, which I have already mentioned, that makes it possible for you to purchase a $500,000 income-producing property with about $100,000 of your own money or a $1,000,000 property with about $200,000. If you can purchase a property that has enough rental income to cover all of the expenses associated with your ownership and still yield a profit, you can truly begin to build your wealth. One feature about owning real estate is that it has favorable tax advantages such as depreciation that allows you to take a tax deduction for something you did not spend money for. A neat thing is that after you own a profit-generating property for twenty years, you owe little or nothing for it, and if you have maintained it well you can sell it for a substantial profit or refinance it and have additional cash to invest in something else. After you become a real estate investor you will learn to find good advisers to help you with the process, including your ownership options, financing, tax treatments, and limiting potential liabilities. Just take care as you delve into all of these activities to fully vet any fiduciaries you plan to work with. You do have to stay informed when dealing with your own hard-earned money and not leave it up to others who can all too easily think of it as monopoly money.

Less understood is the securities market for stocks and bonds because there is more risk and volatility involved. That is compounded by the fact that you are dealing with full-time professionals who are trying to outwit you or take advantage of you. Sometimes it can seem like you're bringing a knife to a gunfight. The stock markets, like politics and gambling, are primarily driven by emotion rather than logic, thus adding another dimension to the risks. Despite these ramifications, securities can be very rewarding investments over time. But there are, again, some basic rules that should be followed to guard against risks.

I once was invited to attend a conference in Scottsdale, Arizona, by *Fortune* magazine because I was the president of a company it had identified as being one of the fastest growing firms in the nation. During the conference, I had lunch with Steve Wiggins, who was the founder and CEO of Oxford Health Care, a company in which I had previously purchased some shares of stock. Wiggins's company was very near the top of the list of fast-growth companies, and I was quite impressed with its history. After returning from the conference I did more research on Oxford, and I purchased additional shares. Every major investment firm and healthcare analysis recommended buying Oxford stock based on its history of expansion and growth. Oxford was one of the most admired companies in the industry. Sometime later, I saw a report that had Oxford's stock priced at about one-third the amount of the previous day's close. "Interesting. They must have had a three-for-one split," I reasoned. Later that day I checked out Oxford's situation. It turned out that Oxford had announced just before the market opened that day that it had to restate the previous year's financial reports because the company had overstated its receivables, the money it was owed, while it had understated its payables, the money Oxford owed others. In short, there had not been a split. Oxford's stock had crashed.

Consequently, the largest single stock loss I ever experienced, over $100,000, involved the company, Oxford Health Care, that I had been the most informed about other than the one I was running myself.

The lesson for you is the one I learned the hard way: That even when stocks appear to be as solid as a rock, they may not be. The other lesson is that extensive research may not provide adequate assurance that a security is worth your investment. I still own securities, but I spread my money over a number of investment options so I am not overexposed in any one area.

If you believe the stock market will increase in value over time, perhaps you should consider a broad-based total market mutual fund that has a low-cost management fee. Fidelity Investments is a good place to start. Open an investment account by putting your money into a money market account, and then spend time learning about stocks. Talk to the people at a Fidelity office. Ask questions. Learn about mutual fund options. While there are sometimes funds that beat the overall stock market average for a brief period of time, there are not many that consistently beat it over the long haul. It is interesting to note that there are more mutual funds available than there are individual stocks listed on the stock exchanges, so you can find a mutual fund that will meet every investment objective you can think of.

Another thing to consider when contemplating stock purchases is that, because of the volatility involved, you want to avoid being forced to sell because you need the money for something else. You should try to keep any funds you might need for something unexpected during the next one or two years in more liquid short-term vehicles, including a money market fund.

I don't want to go into great detail here on investments because I know it will be a few years before you build up your savings to the point of considering these kinds of investments. Furthermore, I realize that once you begin to manage your investments, you will seek out information that will presumably be more relevant to the current economy and markets. And of course you can always talk to your parents or your grandfather.

Finally, you should not overlook the rewards, in terms of economic and personal satisfaction, that comes from owning a business. If you want to be your own boss, then go for it! It can be a great wealth-builder in so many ways. If you can earn enough to live on while operating your own business, you will be building equity in the business itself. That may be much more rewarding economically, as well as personally, than working for someone else. If you are inclined to give it a go, you might just surprise yourself!

About Satisfaction
To be satisfied can be a worthwhile goal

Satisfaction is one of those subjective words that mean different things to different people. You can observe the phenomenon even in really young children. One child can be perfectly content playing with one toy, while another child jumps from one toy to another. An apparently dissatisfied child may even take a toy right out of another child's hands only to discard it a few minutes later. Some people never seem to outgrow that tendency.

You know from your own experiences that the satisfaction derived from obtaining something that you have desired does not last for all that long. We tend to lose interest in something as soon as we own it, even when we had been dreaming about acquiring it for a long time.

There seems to be a part of our nature that causes us to seek changes in just about everything but ourselves. The old joke that "a woman marries a man because she loves him just the way he is, then immediately wants him to change" is absolutely true. Even though we tend to fear change ourselves, we have no reservations about trying to change everything and everybody else. We then call the changes we desire "progress".

I have often wondered just how much progress we have really made because of our meddling and interference that has been based on our dissatisfaction with things as we found them.

I think seriously about our economic system which is based on the ideals of capitalism. The success of capitalism has relied on adding value to things that we originally considered free for the taking – minerals, water, trees, fish, birds, animals, even the air we breathe. Because we thought of these abundant resources as limitless, we developed more and more demand for them to satisfy our civilized needs. Now we are reaching the point of nearly total depletion of just about all of these resources. We kill large game animals for sport, race cars for fun, entertain ourselves with what is called conspicuous consumption, destroy what we find in the natural world to create fashion, and engage in hugely destructive warfare to exercise power over others.

I suspect that many years from now historians will be amazed that we used a precious, valuable, finite resource like fossil fuel to simply burn it, in the same way we now think of how we hunted whales to use their oil in lamps. The constant pursuit of progress, real or perceived, will be an increasingly challenging idea for you and your successors to deal with as the competition intensifies for our decreasing resources. It is not a happy note, but a realistic one. Just think of the added demands by the growing populations of China, India, and all of Africa. History is full of examples whereby competition for finite resources resulted in the total depletion of those resources. Scientists now believe that some of the ancient North American civilizations crashed as a result of over exploitation of their resources. It is imperative that we learn to conserve what we have and stop coveting what we do not need.

Therefore, it is also important that you learn to be satisfied with what you have. Don't covet what others around you have. Most of what we have is stuff we really don't need, even though we believed we just had to have it at the time. Accept the fact that accomplishing major things requires major sacrifices.

Nothing I know of is as satisfying as accomplishing something you have worked very hard at for a long time. I well remember the day I received the letter that informed me I had passed the Massachusetts bar examination and would be sworn in as an attorney. Even now, forty years later, it is still a great source of satisfaction and pride for me. I accomplished that in large measure by myself, with help only from my wife. I had spent nine years and fifty percent of my limited income to get my education while working full time and helping to raise our family. I felt good, and satisfied, about myself because I had earned my membership to the bar.

Graduating to Adulthood

Now I get a great deal of satisfaction from watching the progress my grandchildren are making.

Everyone I know, knows I enjoy Winnie the Pooh. Sometime ago my brother Dennis and his wife Linda gave me a small Penguin book written by Benjamin Hoff titled *The Tao of Pooh*. I highly recommend that you read it. It will make you think about your values and what you need to feel truly satisfied.

About You

In the whole world, there is only one you

It's true. Of the seven billion people on this planet, there is not a single person who is exactly like you. It is a powerful idea. You are indeed unique! Not even identical twins are completely identical. You need not worry about being someone else. You already are. Just by being you, you will always be different. So get used to it!

Now that we understand that each of us is different, we should also understand that we need to relate to most of those differences to function effectively. Being nice to people you meet during your travels and showing interest in them no matter how different they seem to be will make your tasks easier to accomplish. People who are pleasant to those around them and who communicate well are usually highly regarded by their peers. That in turn makes their daily lives much easier and more enjoyable.

There are three things, it is said, that are important to know about real estate: location, location, location. Likewise, there are three important things to know about life: education, education, education. Know who you are. Know that you have no limits in what you can accomplish. And know what you want to focus on to make your life meaningful to yourself.

I have heard it said many times that "it's too bad that youth is wasted on the young." "If I only knew then what I know now" is another common expression. As we age we tend to lament the fact that we did not realize the value of things like education and networking when we were young. It frequently takes time to understand how much other people can help you and how willing they are to do so.

I like the story about Bucky Fuller, a famous inventor, which is related in the book *The Tao of Pooh*. When he was in his early thirties, Fuller lost his daughter, his job, and took to drinking heavily. In the depths of his depression he stood on the bank of Lake Michigan, ready to end his life. As he looked at his image in the water he thought to himself: "Why am I doing this? Why not conduct an experiment to determine how much good one person can do in the world?" He then went on to invent the geodesic dome as an inexpensive way to construct sturdy, reliable buildings.

This true story illustrates the idea that regardless of how hopeless a situation may be, there is reason to be optimistic about your future. Situations can always improve, and the future is always brighter for those who focus on achievement.

I am sure you have learned by now that it is very rewarding to accomplish something you have set out to do. Knowing that, you might assume that most people strive for accomplishments. Yet, that is really not the case. Just look around. People have settled into their routines. They follow the same recipe every day. I call it "attending work."

I have no idea what it is about people that prevents them from seeking achievement. Perhaps they fear failure. Perhaps some lack initiative or motivation because of a medical reason. But surely not everyone is afflicted that way. Most of us do what we are told or have been trained to do. Like ships in a convoy, most of us tend to travel at the same speed. Days go by and little progress appears to be made. Why pick up the pace? Even a convoy eventually reaches its destination.

I do know that our ability to achieve is not based solely on our genes. We are not programmed to succeed any more than we are programmed to fail. The way we live has much to do with our levels of achievement. While living on a farm, I observed that one piglet in a farrow would be smaller than its siblings. It was usually the last one born and could not hold its own at feeding time, meaning it didn't get as much nourishment and, therefore, grew at a slower rate. In that case, food, not genetics, explained the difference in size. Studies have shown that the children of Japanese parents who live in the United States grow taller than the children of relatives in Japan. Again, it's a matter of diet, not genes.

As it is for the body, so it is for the brain. You mind needs to be fed and stimulated to achieve its potential. Please understand, you are not born with genes to be smart or stupid. Your genes obviously may have some predispositions, but they interact with your environment, your diet, and your experiences to bring about who you are. Your genes are not the sole determinant. Life is much more complicated than that. Genes do not act like red or green lights that cannot change colors. While you may not be able to control your gene pool, you do control your everyday activities which in turn are just as important in determining your ability to grow and prosper, to be passive or aggressive, to seek out opportunities, or perhaps, to simply sail in the convoy.

Your mind can be expanded far beyond anything you have thus far experienced. You could spend a lifetime absorbing all there is to know about a subject and not come close to your capacity for learning. What happens more often is that you begin a project and then, in time, lose interest because of familiarity or competing interests. When you go to a place for the first time, you pay attention to everything around you, observing, sometimes excitedly, all that you see. Later, after several visits to that place, you may find yourself not paying attention to your surroundings. You've been there and done that.

When you start a new job, you are alert to everything going on around you. You listen to every word from your new boss. You absorb as much information as you can as quickly as possible. You pay attention to everything you see and hear. You examine your surroundings and the people you meet, trying to remember names and titles and who does what and with whom. You are in a constant state of awareness. During the first six months in a new job, you will probably learn about ninety-five percent of what you will learn during the first six years. The reason is that once you achieve a sufficient level of knowledge about the job and what is expected of you, you let up and begin to coast. After all, you know what you need to do the job. So why do more? And no one is expecting you to do more.

My point is that we frequently fail to achieve as much as we could because we do not always choose to succeed, not because we lack the ability or are deficient in our mental capacity. We have the ability to be whatever we desire to be if we are willing to focus on that single objective and see it through.

Another point I'd like to make is to focus on your strengths, not your weaknesses. Focus on what interests you, what intrigues you, what gets your adrenalin pumping. If you discover you like worms, fish, asteroids, accounting, or corporate law, then focus on that subject and become the most knowledgeable person about it in the world. Challenge yourself to learn more about the subject than the authors of the textbooks. Learn to learn and absorb all you can. I assure you that you will never run out of your capacity to learn. One of my personal regrets is that I will not have enough time to absorb all of the things I want to learn in the mere one hundred years that I expect to be able to study. There is so much information, and it is so intriguing. Understand that I am giving it my best shot. However, as my mother pointed out to me, the challenge as we get older is to learn more each day than we forget.

Every so often someone comes along who is exceptionally different from the norm; someone who by force of personality alone changes the entire world for the good. I admire and envy people like that. I'm thinking of people in my lifetime like Nelson Mandela, Mahatma Gandhi, Martin Luther King, Mother Teresa, and, more recently, Eunice Kennedy Shriver. They used their unique talents to help others. They dedicated their lives to causes they believed in with their whole being. Just like you, they were unique human beings!

(Unfortunately, there have also been leaders like Adolf Hitler, Joseph Stalin and Chairman Mao who used their talents primarily to destroy others.)

You have to challenge yourself to be a doer and not settle into a sedate, routine life. It is hard to imagine anything more rewarding than helping others and making this world a better place. As a very special and unique individual, with talents and skills that reside solely in you, with experiences that only you have lived, you can add a special something to our world during your lifetime that no one else can contribute.

So I urge you to dream, set your goals, and then pursue them with tenacity. Trust your vibes. Navigate using your values and dreams as your compass.

Another thing you must remember and never once forget: Your integrity is your personal currency in life. It is what you use to establish your credibility with your family, your friends, your colleagues, and your community at large. Your reputation and integrity, like the pyramids, takes years to build and can be destroyed in seconds. A person's word must be his or her bond. There really must be trust at some level between people who deal with one another. In the past, it was common for people to conduct business based solely on oral agreements or promises – on their word. Diamond merchants still conduct all of their business with each other without any paperwork – with strictly oral commitments. Every person in the chain is completely trusted by everyone else because it is known that if one breaks his word with anyone, the bond will be broken with all, and the offending person will be ostracized by the entire industry.

If you compromise your integrity, it may take many years to regain it. And you may never regain it at all. So guard it well!

About Faith
An unquestioned belief

When I began second grade in Fitchburg, Massachusetts, I would leave the house every morning and walk three blocks to the Hosmer Elementary School. At least that's what my mother thought.

Actually, I would stop and play, often in a sandbox, with a little red-headed girl who lived about halfway between my home and the school. Charlie Brown never had it so good. What I liked most about the little red-headed girl was that she had lots of small toys, including planes and trucks, which I could play with. I would fly those planes and drive those trucks wherever my imagination would take me. It was so much more interesting and fun than going to school.

My daily routine was not interrupted until close to Thanksgiving when my teacher showed up on our doorstep to deliver a get-well card, inquire about my health, and give my mother a fruit basket purchased with contributions from my classmates. It seems that when I didn't show up at school, my brother David, who was in kindergarten, would be asked if I was sick. Since he couldn't think of anything to say, he nodded yes. By the end of October my teacher assumed I must be seriously ill and came to visit.

That was followed by a brief time when, to put it delicately, my mother and especially my father impressed upon me the importance of going to school. My father decided I had to be taught a lesson about doing the right thing, so he took off his belt and told me he would use it on my backside. Then, after giving me a few minutes to let the fear sink in, he said his belt wouldn't hurt enough so he was going to get a razor strop from the barber. A razor strop was made of thick leather, about three inches wide, used to hone straight razors for shaving.

By the time my father returned with that leather strop, I can assure you I had already fully resolved to never skip school again. My father ordered me to go down to the cellar, drop my pants, and bend over. I was shaking at the thought of that great big strop hitting my backside. And when he did hit me I screamed like he was killing me. The truth was, however, that the strop looked more frightening than it really was. Its width spread the blow over a large surface of my backside, and it really didn't hurt that badly. My father knew that, but the psychology of the tactic had its desired effect.

However, I had already missed so much school that I had to repeat second grade. Furthermore, the situation led to new school policies requiring parents or guardians to provide valid reasons for their children missing school. So even at a young age, I uncovered an administrative oversight and made a contribution to improving our educational system.

Without realizing it, skipping school was an early lesson for me about faith as well as duty and honor. Faith, in that my parents did not give me logical reasons about why I had to attend school. They convinced me to believe in their good judgment. Duty, in that it was my responsibility as the oldest child in my family to set a proper example for my younger siblings. Honor, in that I respected my parents' desire for me to attend.

I'm going to offer you a somewhat different slant on the values of faith than what you might expect.

The definition of faith can be simply stated: "Belief without proof."

Faith, to most, means religion. There are many different ideas about who or what God is and who or what God isn't. What people believe in has evolved over the ages based on cultural, geographic, and political influences. Islam and Christianity, two of the largest religions, were largely spread as a result of military power. We now have dedicated followers for a multitude of Christian denominations, Islam, Hinduism, Buddhism, Judaism, Taoism, Sikhism, Confucianism, Scientism, and on and on – all with significantly or slightly differing beliefs. Some, such as Mormonism as it is practiced in this country and Jainism in India, are relatively new, having been organized during the past few centuries. Some, such as the Australian Aboriginal people's belief in multiple deities that exist in such places as rocks, rivers, and depressions in the ground, are very old. Almost all believe that their religion is the one true religion.

Today we can find many people, in politics and even in science, who have formed beliefs that are clearly not founded on evidence or facts but on an unquestioned confidence in their own knowledge. You can observe people you know, perhaps even yourself, who frequently disregard as total trash information they do not agree with, while information they do agree with tends to reinforce their existing beliefs and opinions. In both situations, the information may not have been objectively challenged and may not be factual or represent the truth.

That is why, in some respects, comparing loyalties to a political party and to a religious belief may be entirely valid. For many, both forms of loyalty rely on belief without proof. Interestingly, when a political organization or a religion is under pressure and losing followers, the members blame outside forces of evil and press their loyal adherents to redouble their efforts to reinvigorate the population and win converts.

There is no proof that God exists. Nor is there proof that God does not exist. Atheists, agnostics and religious practitioners can offer evidence to support their beliefs, but not proof.

It seems so confusing, all of these different religions and faith-based behaviors. Why should it make a difference to you or me? Does it mean we should throw up our hands in despair? Of course not!

The bottom line seems to indicate a universal theme in religious faiths; that those who believe should respect others and perform good deeds. Be good. Those who do so are rewarded in an afterlife. In addition, there must be some reason why, throughout human history, mankind has sought a greater meaning and sense of purpose in our existence and has even formulated similar thoughts about our preferred behavior.

Furthermore, I would suggest that many mysteries remain in the physical sciences and biology despite the pursuit of solutions by many generations of brilliant minds; so it is not a big deal that mysteries about our religions remain hidden as well. If you were born in Ireland, you would most likely identify yourself as a Roman Catholic. If you were born in Saudi Arabia, you would say you were a follower of Islam. In India you would be a Hindu; in Thailand a Buddhist. Where you were born and what religion your parents practiced is the biggest influence on your religious beliefs. It is a gift from your parents!

Don't let the unknown elements hold you back. Adopting a religion does have an upside. Having a God can help you achieve a sense of purpose in your life. And if you can talk to your God, it will definitely give you peace of mind in dealing with your world. Something in our humanity seeks a spiritual element to our existence. What I'm suggesting is that the endless seeking of proof of a God's existence may not really be necessary. If it feels right and causes no harm or injury, then why not embrace it? Enjoy the upside.

You already know that when you practice your religion and attend services you are reminded of your responsibilities to yourself and others in the community. It reinforces the notion that happiness involves trust in other people; and you have hopefully discovered that your bonds with those you love are strengthened by that trust.

About Emotions
Hearts overrule minds

I believe that every major decision you will make during your life will be influenced primarily by your emotions rather than by logic. In fact, you will develop logical arguments following your actions to lend credibility to your emotion-driven decisions.

We want to "justify" our choices. For some reason, we feel a need to suppress or deny our "subjective" decisions, which are most often based on our emotions, in favor of our desire to make "objective" choices.

It is not quite as easy as it sounds to analyze a situation objectively and then translate that analysis into a rational action. Take something as simple as selecting a personal communication device, commonly known as a telephone. I'm sure you have one that, when you bought it, best suited your needs. It had the features, functions, and benefits you thought you required based on your analysis of your potential usage, however casual that analysis may have been. The way the telephone looked, the influence of your peers, or the manufacturer's advertising campaigns had nothing to do with your selection, right? It was the logical choice! At least that's what you told yourself.

One of the most difficult challenges we repeatedly encounter is maintaining a balance between our self-interests and self-desires. Self-interests are the actions that promote our well-being and move us along a path of desirable progress. Self-desires usually only satisfy a perceived short-term need. Unfortunately, for just about all of us, the self-desires that are driven by our emotions have the edge. Those are the decisions that get us into trouble, such as using our credit cards to purchase items – stuff – that we don't need but that seem so necessary at the time. Merchants take advantage of our propensity to make hasty self-desirous decisions with tempting displays at the ends of isles or near the checkout counters. It's called "impulse buying." You decide on impulse that you want it, and before you can change your mind you own it.

Impulse buying is a universal trait that is not greatly affected by people's incomes. Most people, except for the ones at the very bottom of the economic ladder whose only concern is survival, buy goods and services on impulse – from a fine dinner to a fancy car. You can argue that the entire global luxury goods industry is a self-desirous or self-want industry. Clearly, outrageously expensive watches and jewelry, automobiles such as Lamborghinis, and mega-million-dollar mansions are self-want items. But on close examination you will find that much of what you want, and may already have, while certainly not as ostentatious as the aforementioned, are self-want items as well. Think of all the options, the bells and whistles, which you have purchased with cars or TVs or, indeed, that personal communication device.

The difference between impulsive decisions and most other decisions is the element of time. The shorter the time between the idea and the action, the more likely it will be for self-desire and the less likely it will be for self-interest. That is one reason why you should use the element of time to assist you when making many of your decisions. If you decide to purchase something expensive, resolve that you will not make a commitment the first time you visit the merchant; that you will instead fact-find and gather as much information as you can to compare and consider the alternatives. And there are always alternatives. This technique will help you resist the temptations of making costly commitments you may come to regret. Another idea is to look at these expensive items as if they were a house where you plan to live for many years. Do you really think that the car you are looking at will best suit your needs five years from now?

Time is one element that marketers will try to use against you. Many resorts and other vacation spots have kiosks or desks where salespeople urge you to sign up for free meals or other enticements to get you to attend an informational presentation about the resort or its affiliates. When you attend you find yourself sitting with someone whose job it is to get as much information about you as possible and to introduce you to the idea of buying a timeshare. If you are reluctant to purchase, that person will introduce you to another person who, armed with the information the first person has gleaned from you, will push hard to close the deal. You will likely hear something like this: "If you sign up today you are entitled to a special rate." The idea is to get you to act right now. The same strategy is used in selling automobiles and furniture. I'm sure you know that you could easily get the same deal tomorrow or the day after. Time in these situations is critical only to the salespeople who are looking to earn their commissions. I suggest that you not waste your time by accepting these free lunches to begin with. The old saying that "you can't get something for nothing" is absolutely true.

However, buying stuff, no matter how expensive, is truly insignificant compared to the really important decisions you will make during your life or that you have perhaps already made. I'm talking about the decisions regarding other people. Because now it's emotions dealing with emotions!

It seems as if every major company I have gotten to know has gone to great lengths to ensure that new hires and promotions were based on objective criteria. The companies recognized the importance of selecting the best people for the jobs. So checklists were developed and multiple inputs were sought in an effort to make sure the very best talent available was selected. Human resource departments still spend enormous amounts of time and energy developing meaningful analytical tools. In reality, however, all of these attempts at objectivity are thwarted by human nature. In the end, it really is who knows who, who has a compatible personality, and who the boss is most comfortable with. In other words, just about all hires and promotions are based on subjective and not objective reasoning. That is one reason why a strong-willed boss is usually surrounded by "yes" men and women. Despite all of the concerted efforts to logically select the best candidates, in the end, even in business, emotions reign.

How many times have you met a couple and wondered what they see in each other? The two individuals seem to be totally oblivious to what, to you, are obvious differences. You are puzzled by the fact that one party seems to be totally blind to the reality of who his or her partner truly is. You may be friends with couples that you just know are headed for an unhappy coexistence if they remain together. Unfortunately, some of those relationships might even end in tragedy.

Those people are trapped by their past emotions. It is not uncommon that we develop a loyalty to our emotions. You meet someone and in time form an emotional bond with that person. When it turns out that the person is not the individual you were originally attracted to or felt you just had to be with, you are faced with what can be a very painful and difficult decision. You can either divorce yourself from your original emotional tie by backing off from your close relationship with that person, or you can choose to make an effort to cling to your relationship out of a loyalty to your original emotions.

Like so many other experiences in life, this can lead to extremes. How sad it is to be aware of people who are in abusive relationships with other people. It is many times sadder when the abused party seems to accept it as being his or her lot in life. Often the abused parties cling to the idea that it is somehow their fault, that they have done something that justifies the abusive behavior. They nurture early memories of the person they fell in love with, and they convince themselves that things will get better because they know their abuser is "really not like that." Often there is an unfounded belief that the abuser will change and the situation will get better.

If you are not currently bonded in a relationship with a significant other, you need to know just how much your emotions can cover up the true nature of someone else. I'm not suggesting that you refrain from reaching out or enjoying the company of others, but I am suggesting that you make an effort to fully understand, through self-examination, who you are to the point where you can test your emotional responses with a reality check.

If you are in a relationship, I'm sure you will agree that it is equally important for you to understand the other person's true character. Set aside the rose-colored glasses and really take a hard look at your friend, closely examining just how compatible the two of you really are.

I should add that it gets complicated because your wants and needs are not static. Let me remind you that you both are in a constant state of flux, though less so as you age, with the biggest changes occurring during your twenties and early thirties. You will tend to settle down at some point and essentially be "who you are." We are creatures of habit, and those habits do become more ingrained with age.

As I have mentioned in other parts of this book, there is no better emotion than the pleasure you derive from loving another person. Nothing – not money, not success in business, not achieving a long-sought goal – can eclipse the rewarding emotion that your love for another person can provide. It is incredible!

And if you are to share in this most magnificent of all emotions, it is incumbent on you to understand what is truly in your own heart as well as in the heart of the person of your attention. Because of the significant impact these emotions can have on your entire life, you have to be very sure of where your self-desires and self-interests are leading you and be able to clearly distinguish between them.

Be aware of just how strong these emotional feelings can be and how these feelings can sometimes lead you to see things that do not exist. Too many people live in a fantasy world created by their emotional needs. Please don't be one of them! Remind yourself that you do in fact have a rational side that needs to be brought to bear, especially when contemplating major decisions that will have a long-term impact on your life.

There will, however, be times – despite all of my precautionary words about controlling your emotions – when every vibe in your body tells you to proceed; when in your heart you just know it is the right thing to do. Then do it!

About Mistakes

Don't be afraid to make mistakes. Learn, then move on

We often hear the expression "You learn from your mistakes." In most cases it is true that we should learn from our mistakes. But sometimes, even when we have learned a lesson, it is of little use to us. It may, in fact, even be harmful because we have absorbed the wrong lesson from our experience.

On the whole, however, the expression is correct. In my case, the sooner I made the mistakes, the better off I was. Unfortunately, I made some of my biggest mistakes far too many years after I needed to learn from them. So timing has a great deal to do with the value of what we learn from our mistakes. I have so few regrets in my life, but oh how I wish I made more of those big mistakes sooner!

But I did learn from my mistakes whenever they occurred, and I learned something further. You need to use your mistakes as opportunities to learn, but you also need to learn to ignore the mistakes themselves after you have learned the lessons. If you are unable to set aside your mistakes, they will become anchors that will slow down your progress. If you can't pull in those anchors, they will prevent you from moving on.

To clarify, the term "mistakes" is a euphemism that applies to a whole range of actions: perhaps deliberately doing something you know you shouldn't but doing it anyway, or rationalizing not being truthful, or just doing something incredibly stupid.

Perhaps the biggest obstacle in our lives is our fear of making a mistake in the first place. We fear doing something wrong. We worry about what other people will think about us if we try and do not succeed because we make a mistake. We start creating doubts in our minds by thinking: "What if I miss the ball?" "What if I fail?"

"Boy, will they think I'm dumb." "What if the boss finds out?" "How will it look?" Our ego is often on the line. Most of us have an image of ourselves that we want to protect. Having to admit to a mistake, we believe, tarnishes that image.

Often, the bottom-line lesson we learn is to avoid anything risky that might lead to more mistakes. So we play it safe. That's why many people become more adverse to risks as they grow older.

So what were my big mistakes, and what did I learn from them? (I can't tell you about all of my mistakes because my memory isn't that good, and it would take at least eight hundred more pages.)

Perhaps the most significant events in my life were getting married and fathering children long before I was emotionally or financially prepared to do so. These were actions I had not planned for or even seriously considered. Not that I didn't act responsibly when they occurred, but our circumstances were much more difficult than they might have been had I given them even a small amount of forethought. That was my mistake.

I learned some tough lessons. I learned that I was no longer solely accountable to myself. I now bore the responsibility of supporting a family, both financially and as a role model. I had to consider others before acting. I was now required to work full time. I could no longer consider going to college as a traditional student. I had to nearly abandon many of my friends and members of our extended family because I no longer had the time to spend with them.

Clearly, you should not enter a marriage cavalierly. It is an extremely complex situation. And despite what the romantics say, money can and does make a difference. With adequate financial resources, there are fewer potential problems. The lesson to be passed on is that there truly is no need to enter into a lifelong commitment until you understand the responsibilities and consequences and are somewhat prepared to meet them.

Another lesson I learned from all of this is that time actually works against you. It is much wiser to establish your economic base during your twenties and to learn how real maturity benefits your personal relationships. It is amazing how much your tastes change in all kinds of things between the ages of twenty and thirty. Besides your improved tastes in dress and food, you will develop a greater appreciation for, among other things, finer furniture and art. You will look at things you acquired ten years earlier and ask yourself why you ever liked them.

It might help to think about your life as if you were constructing a building.

The first thing you need is a good foundation. If you are planning a long and productive life, you have to build a solid base. Education and financial planning are your major building blocks. Focus on saving money and avoiding expenses. Concentrate on what you need, not on what you want.

The more you can save and invest during your twenties, the better prepared you will be to deal with the rest of your life's economic demands. You will, no doubt, become a disciplined saver by the time you reach thirty. You will have learned the value of accumulating wealth and the incredible power of compound interest.

Compound interest is what makes a wise investment double in value in seven or eight years and double again in another seven and so on until, after thirty-five years, a $2,000 investment is worth $64,000; and after forty-two years it's worth $128,000. That is why, if you follow the pay-yourself rule when you begin working, you will be a multimillionaire when you choose to retire.

Just as important, if you begin saving seriously during your twenties, you will learn by the time you are thirty that the key to saving is to control, reduce, or, if possible, avoid spending money entirely. That means no impulse buying – except for an occasional ice cream cone.

I hope you will learn that financing anything is a costly way to buy it. The worst of all situations is to finance something that depreciates in value, such as a car or a major household appliance. If you pay cash for your car, two things will happen. First, after you save enough money to make the purchase, you will realize how much you value that money and you will tend to select a less expensive automobile. Second, you will not buy new because of the rapid depreciation. Too often, when someone finances a new car, they are inclined to add upgrades they do not really need because it is so easy to rationalize paying a few more dollars per month.

When you finance anything, you are mortgaging your future. Think about the implications of that! By limiting your available resources, you are restricting your options for the future. Remember, your objective should be to build a foundation that is solid enough to support what you want to do for the rest of your life.

Another major lesson I have learned involves my nature to always be optimistic. I seldom experience a bad day. When asked how I am, I always respond: "Super," "Fantastic," "Terrific," or even "Phantasmagorical." And believe it or not, I always mean it!

Optimism in and of itself is not bad. But optimism must be based on real-world assessments of facts, not fantasies. Otherwise, it can lead to disaster. Many times my optimism has been fueled by my ego. Often, because of my optimistic outlook on life, I assumed I was smarter than I really was. I just didn't know what I didn't know. Often it was because I didn't assess my knowledge about a subject as thoroughly as I should have. One of my law school professors cautioned that if we thought a problem on an examination was easy, we probably did not fully understand the question and might fail the test.

Another of my major faults is to misjudge people, because I prefer to assume everyone is good and has good intentions. We are, however, all different. As the author Bill Bryson commented in his book *A Short History of Nearly Everything,* being different is the only thing we all have in common. We are the sum of our experiences and environments mixed in with our genetics. To be fair to all, I especially try to judge people in the business community by their accomplishments, not by their quirks and foibles. I have not always succeeded at that, however, because emotion sometimes overrules logic and objectivity in human affairs.

Experience has taught me the painful lesson that all people are not good and do not have good intentions. It's another way of saying that I've been burned many times. I have dealt with a few people who were very good at concealing who they really were. Unfortunately, many of these individuals were acting as fiduciaries. Many times I placed my trust in someone who abused or misused that trust. These were just plain bad judgments on my part, and I don't want you to make similar mistakes. My word to the wise is to be careful whom you trust.

The related challenge for me is to not let one person's dishonesty keep me from treating others with the respect they deserve. Deep down I think good things will happen to good people, so naturally I try to be good. My advice to you is that, as difficult as it may seem at the time, you will be much more fulfilled and satisfied if you don't hold grudges or bemoan the fact that you were not treated fairly. Hey, sometimes life is not fair. Get over it!

In terms of my career, some of my early mistakes had to do with my self-confidence and my resultant failure to seek out competent experts for advice; and not understanding the power of delegating.

When it comes to self-confidence, we all go through periods when we feel good about ourselves and periods when we are less optimistic about what we can accomplish. We drift into melancholy moods and loose our lust for our everyday lives. It took me some time after I graduated from law school to realize that I was working with people who had two distinct types of knowledge and that I was just as competent as any of my peers. When I focused on something, I generally caught on quickly and could get up to speed in a very short time. I could really laser in on a subject.

The two types of knowledge my co-workers possessed were (1) expertise in a narrow field of endeavor such as government contracts, cost accounting, an engineering discipline, or a manufacturing or quality assurance process or (2) information about a wide range of disciplines. Since I knew I usually had a short attention span for things, I deduced that I was better suited for the latter category. However, I did resolve to gain an in-depth knowledge about a subject when the situation required.

Remember, I did not get my business degree until I was twenty-eight or my law degree until I was thirty-two. Most of my peers in the professional workforce, with whom I had to compete, had gone to college immediately after high school and had their undergraduate degrees when they were twenty-two and their law degrees or MBAs by twenty-five. They had a significant head start on me in the business world and were about a fifth of the way around the track when I first stepped onto it.

Furthermore, I got off to a slow start because I was initially intimidated by other people's resumes and hesitated to compete with them. In the beginning I was a bit reticent about dealing with someone on the other side of the table who had a law degree or MBA from Harvard or Yale. There I was, a small-town boy who had gotten his education at night school. I hesitated because I wondered how I could possibly compete with people who went to some of the most prestigious schools in the country. Well, it soon became clear to me that I could compete with those people. And I did! It's at those times when something called "hunger" sets in, and I was hungry for success.

Think about how you want to approach your career. Do you want to develop a special expertise in a field of your interest, or would you prefer to run your own company or maybe somebody else's? Please understand that there is no reason for you not to do what you have a passion to do; that the people you are being compared to or competing against or working with as peers are not any smarter than you are. Therefore, you should not hesitate to have all the confidence in the world in yourself and in your abilities. As I previously mentioned, tenacity can be the great equalizer. It's the great power of perseverance.

Just because you know that someone is a lawyer doesn't mean you should engage that person if you have no objective way of learning about his or her level of competence. You need to spend the time to properly vet anyone you are going to place in a position of trust. Remember that business is business and friendship is friendship and, like religion and politics, the two should be kept separate. I write from experience because I broke that rule and suffered as a consequence. It just doesn't pay to always be a nice guy. In fact, it can be quite costly to be a nice guy when searching for competent personnel. If the results are truly important to you, then make sure you have applied your best assets to the situation. Try hard to find the very best people in their fields when you are choosing the people you plan to depend on for advice or otherwise represent you. Striving for excellence is critical. This is not an area in which you want to compromise.

Another one of my mistakes had to do with my personality. Because I didn't want to impose, I found it difficult to ask other people to do things for me. Sometimes I thought it was "my work," and I felt guilty about having others do it for me. It took me far too long to realize that I had to delegate the workload to be an effective manager. Delegating was a big part of my job. If someone else didn't understand how a task had to be done, my job was to make sure they knew how to do it, not to do it myself. So my advice to you is to delegate early and delegate often. Take care, however, to provide clear and concise instructions so you get the results you desire.

About Success
You need to define your own success

It's true. You have the power to define what you consider success or failure for your life. It is, therefore, up to you to choose what you believe is the appropriate yardstick for measuring yourself.

Throughout this book I have chronicled my thoughts and recommendations about various elements of success. People all around you will be prone to measure or compare your success with theirs. They will use what they believe to be the proper yardstick, which can vary considerably depending on the individuals and their backgrounds. A mega-millionaire would probably consider material wealth as the ultimate sign of success. A street thug might define success as becoming a made man in the Mafia. To an actor, landing the lead role in a Broadway play might be the pinnacle of success. To a fighter pilot, it could be blasting an enemy out of the sky or flying with the Blue Angels.

It is up to you to define your own criteria for success based on wealth or education or family or professional accomplishments.

Many people over the years have complimented me on my success because they assumed that after climbing the corporate ladder I achieved wealth. They are correct in that I have enjoyed a privileged lifestyle for many years because I received a more than adequate income and accumulated some wealth because of many years of disciplined saving. While I will not deny a certain amount of pride in my accomplishments, I know that I benefited from the help of many others and a certain amount of luck. You need not try to copy me, however. I believe there are many others whose footsteps you should consider following.

Let me offer you the examples of two people whom I personally admire and see as being exceptionally successful. These are men I highly recommend you try to emulate. To me they represent the ideal. They achieved happy, satisfying, and – by most measures – totally successful lives by following a simple formula of hard, dedicated work. I have observed these two people and their families for more than six decades, and I love them dearly.

Interestingly, both men have much in common. While they are two very different people who pursued two very different professions, they have shared nearly identical life experiences. They each have remained married to a woman they love deeply, treat as an equal, and acknowledge as their best friend. They confide in their partner about everything. Their spouse is their closest confidant and advisor.

Both men were born to poor families, but from the time of their youth they never flinched at or shied away from hard work or long hours. Both began their careers by working for other firms, but they subsequently became owners of their own businesses. Interestingly, both still live in the first houses they ever purchased. They made some modest renovations, but only after they had accumulated a comfortable amount of wealth. And both accumulated their wealth over many years by living below what their income allowed. Both also took their children's educations very seriously, and all of their children have graduated from some of the finest universities in the land.

Because they became so accomplished as professionals and successful in business, and because they never moved, each man became a well-known and respected community leader and role model. I am not alone in holding these two men in the highest esteem, and I encourage you to learn from and follow their examples. Both of these men are extremely gracious and are easily approachable.

Who are these two men I admire so much?

The first is my brother-in-law, Nicholas Dominic Mercadante. The second is my brother, John Henry Gravelle.

Nick Mercadante grew up in a small house on the steep side of a hill in the Italian section of Worcester, Massachusetts. His parents came from the town of Lacedonia in central Italy, about halfway between Naples and Bari. Nick was a good student and attended the

College of the Holy Cross in Worcester where he majored in accounting. He laid railroad track during one summer to help pay for his education.

Nick began his career with a small accounting firm in Athol after graduating from college. His strong work ethic and attention to detail earned him a great deal of respect among his clients in the Athol area. Later, after taking the plunge and starting his own accounting practice, many of those clients went with him even though he was located twenty-five miles away in Fitchburg. His business grew slowly at first. Then it picked up considerably as his reputation grew in the community. Eventually he was asked to serve on the board of directors for Fitchburg Savings Bank (now Rollstone Bank and Trust) and was subsequently elected chairman of the board.

Nick practices what he preaches. Early on, he dedicated himself to providing his children with the best education and opportunities for financial success he could. He knew it meant a life of material sacrifice for him and his wife Frances. Nick always set the bar high for himself and for his children. They all rose to the challenge and earned degrees from the Ivy League's University of Pennsylvania and advanced degrees from other fine schools.

My brother John was the fifth of my parents' ten children. From a very young age, John was both industrious and imaginative. If there is a common trait in our family, it is the willingness to work long and hard and to look for every opportunity to do so. All of us worked a myriad of odd jobs after school and during the summers. When John was about twelve, he was piloting a passenger ferryboat around Lake Whalom while the captain enjoyed the ride.

After graduating from Lunenburg High School, John went to work as an apprentice in a machine shop. When working as a certified machinist, he made the jump to become a tool and die maker. That work required greater precision and a more sophisticated knowledge base. After working at one of the larger companies in the area, John went to work for his father-in-law in a small four-man shop. During the evenings, he learned how to read and build things from blueprints and how to estimate jobs for customers.

John became increasingly involved in the business after his father-in-law developed bone cancer. John then ran the business for his mother-in-law after her husband died and, eventually, bought the business. He accomplished that because he had impeccable credit, no debts other than a small mortgage, and already had some savings that early in his career.

Over the years John significantly expanded the Mar-Lee business. It did not grow on automatic pilot. It grew because of deliberate, sometimes bold business decisions that John made to build a better future for the company and his family. John never lost sight of his mission. Thanks to his attention to detail and insatiable curiosity he became a master of both his trade and his business.

I once accompanied John to a meeting with top executives of the largest manufacturer of injection molding machines in the world. The man in charge of engineering pulled me aside and asked if John had gone to MIT or some other highly regarded technological college. The man was that impressed with John's grasp of the technology and his comprehension of the fine points of precision molding.

Mar-Lee was not always profitable. But when it was, the money stayed in the business to support John's long-range plans. John sold the business to a French company in 2008, and in 2009 he started a consulting business to stay engaged in the things he liked to do. Then, in 2011, he became the principal owner of Sterling Manufacturing Company. John works for the sheer enjoyment of it.

John and his wife, Sheila, expected discipline and performance from their children when it came to education. Their two sons were excellent students who now hold degrees from esteemed colleges and are enjoying successful careers. Furthermore, John practiced what he preached. He recognized that wealth must be accumulated, and he kept his expenses below his income during his entire working life to accomplish wealth-building.

I have always admired both of these men for their tenacity and integrity. Nick and John played the game without cheating. They earned everything they have. Both can hold their heads high because they made the best of their circumstances and dealt with whatever fate had in store for them without compromising their values or their good names.

You cannot go wrong in using Nick or John as a role model. They are two of the most worthy people I know.

Your own success, then, will be defined by you, timed largely by you, and ultimately achieved by you; but always with the assistance of others. Understand what it is you want, when you want it, and whether you are prepared to pay the price to achieve your idea of success.

About Democracy
Citizenship is a duty

You live in a country that was established as a republic, a representative democracy. The people who wrote the key documents establishing our government were themselves representatives of people living in thirteen British colonies along the Eastern seaboard. When we vote for political candidates, we are asking them to be our eyes and ears in government, representing us as best they can, using their best judgment on the issues that come before them.

The concept of democracy as we know it was initiated by the Athenians during the middle of the first millennium BCE, well over two thousand years ago. In historical terms, their experiment with this new concept of government was short-lived. The Romans tried it a few hundred years later, but, like the Greek experience, it also soon floundered and died. In both instances, citizens and leaders alike participated in the destruction of individual freedoms.

Since the American Revolution that brought forth our democratic nation, several other countries have embarked on a similar course. It is interesting to note that not all of the people who tried a democratic form of government were able to sustain it, at least initially. Some, like France after its revolution, the newly democratic Republic of China under Sun Yat-sen in 1911, Germany from the end of World War I until 1933, and the Russians under Alexander Kerensky, soon abandoned democracy for dictatorships, which subsequently led to considerable hardships for a majority of the people.

Winston Churchill once observed: "It has been said that Democracy is the worst form of government except all those other forms that have been tried from time to time." While I don't think that any form of government is without its problems, I do think it is worthwhile to be aware of the current issues, to look for opportunities, and to try to resolve problems.

Just because a government is democratic does not mean it is necessarily a good one or that it supports the right things. One thing that all democratic nations throughout history, including our own, have had in common is the attitude that their causes are just because they have been supported by a majority of the people. The Greeks, Romans, British, and Americans, for example, all believed in the right of slavery at some time in their histories.

Another example involves the imposition of external force by a democracy as opposed to many governments that focus on internal force. Mao Zedong, who ultimately led the Communist Party to victory in China, said in 1938: "Every Communist must grasp the truth: Political power grows out of the barrel of a gun."

Mao was wrong. Political power is derived from controlling the resources that make the guns!

China is now in the process of learning that lesson. When nations move from an agrarian to an industrial base, predictable patterns of change occur. Urban centers grow as the population shifts from the farms to the cities. Industrialists receive support from capitalists and in turn exploit their advantages. Labor abuses become common, worker safety is not given a high priority, environmental pollution increases dramatically, and overcrowding occurs along with lax housing and health standards. And, oh yes, corruption occurs on a large scale because the practitioners have not learned the refined techniques of democratically changing the rules.

When industry expands, it creates and uses capital (money). Capital is provided by financial institutions that are essentially created by clever businessmen who in turn provide capital to other businessmen. These people become the wealthy "barons" who control both the financial and industrial empires.

Many such people and their institutions are agile and therefore move much faster than governments and policymakers can. Thus, a wide gap exists between capitalist activities and public policy. It is not until social activism and the resulting upheaval occurs that the gap can be narrowed to an acceptable level. As I explained in the chapter "About Rules," the government never does catch up entirely.

As China undergoes its transition, we constantly hear complaints from Western business people that China does not play fair, that it does not follow international business and trade rules. If you look back at the experience of the United States during the nineteenth and twentieth centuries, you can see in China a strong resemblance to many of our own experiences dealing with the rapid changes brought on by industrialization and the emergence of capitalism. There is a need for enforceable laws dealing with labor rights, property rights, education, safety, the environment, health care, and the establishment of a fair and equal rule of law for all citizens. I predict there will be many scandals and injustices involving wealthy businessmen, politicians, and citizens in China's future. They will be among China's growing pains.

Both China and the United States, and indeed many other countries, are facing similar challenges with governance. Can their citizens maintain a level of awareness to ensure that their governments remain responsible to the majority of those citizens? It is one of your primary duties as citizens to stay informed and to encourage others to do the same. In our democracy especially, we strive to exercise the will of the majority with the least harm to the minority. This is one of our core beliefs. Without your participation, your voice will not be heard. Your lack of involvement could very well be harmful to your fellow citizens as well as to you. You do need to be involved in our participatory democracy. I recommend that you reread the Declaration of Independence and the Constitution of the United States every five years to refresh your memories. They are incredible documents!

When our forefathers wrote the Constitution, one of the most unique features they included was the separation of powers. It was James Madison's idea that three branches – legislative, executive and judicial – govern the nation, with the executive and legislative branches directly accountable to the electorate. The forefathers agreed to the separation of responsibilities to avoid weaknesses or abuses of power that existed in other governments at the time. Importantly, the system safeguards the equality and ideals proclaimed in the Declaration of Independence to protect minorities from being overrun by majorities.

Most states in turn established their governments with the same separation of powers. Counties and cities followed suit by establishing their own levels of executives (commissioners or mayors), legislative bodies (city councils) and judicial systems (municipal courts). After more than two hundred years, separation of power at many levels has morphed into a situation wherein many governmental agencies and departments possess greater negative power than positive power. These are the many organizations from which approvals or permits are needed before some form of individual action can be taken. Most of these groups or agencies do not or cannot initiate any positive action, but they can effectively establish roadblocks for those who try. Zoning boards do not propose projects. They can approve the ones they want and reject the ones they don't. Much of this behavior is driven by human nature and occurs in just about every large organization, so it is not unique to the USA.

You will find much to complain about in America, in the cities and towns, counties and states where there are always issues of contention that may seem stupid or petty. But unless you take some action to influence those issues, you are in no position to criticize the results. You have an obligation to know who represents you in the local, state, and federal governments. It is important that you make your voice heard during elections and with policy-making bodies. It is a serious responsibility passed on to you by the brilliant framers of our Constitution and the millions before you who have worked and sacrificed to ensure your right to a just and free government.

I should caution you, however, that just because so many before you have worked, even sacrificed their lives, for these ideals does not mean that your rights to life, liberty, and the pursuit of happiness, as stated in the Declaration of Independence, have been guaranteed. As magnificent as our Constitution is, it can still be subverted. What you believe to be your rights can be taken away.

How?

Need I remind you of the actions taken by all three major branches of our government since 9/11? Before then we had few restrictions on what we could carry onto an airplane, our telephone conversations were not monitored by government agencies, our ability to travel overseas was not controlled by a federal agency that now employs a couple of hundred thousand people, no American citizen could be arrested and held without charges for an indefinite period of time, and our country did not routinely torture prisoners. Some of you are too young to fully appreciate the changes that 9/11 brought to our shores and the paranoia about security it created, but it wouldn't take much research to get a good idea.

If you look back to the Second World War, you will find that many American citizens of Japanese descent were rounded up and confined in large camps for the duration of the war because, unlike our citizens of German ancestry, they looked different. They were denied their constitutional rights because the prejudicial and political pressures placed on our executive and legislative officers were sufficient to make them compromise their respect for our Constitution with regard to Japanese-American citizens. And the judicial branch did not prevent that breach of liberty from occurring. Now we are witnessing a concerted effort by moneyed interests to influence the political process involved in selecting our judiciary. This effort, coupled with other pressures from religious and radical left and rightwing organizations, does not bode well for individual rights.

So the bottom line is that the people who represent and govern you can and sometimes will infringe upon your liberties and may even take away your individual freedoms that the Constitution supposedly guarantees. It may even be accomplished with the support of the people. Adolf Hitler became the leader of Nazi Germany because he convinced a majority of Germans to ignore facts and act on nationalistic emotions fueled by fear. Those forces are always close to the surface when times are hard. People are attracted to simple-sounding answers for complex problems, and nothing is more complex than government.

In 1860, James Russell Lowell wrote in *The Atlantic* magazine: "The true danger to popular form of government begins when public opinion ceases because people are incompetent or unwilling to think. In a democracy it is the duty of every citizen to think; but unless the thinking results in a definite opinion, and the opinion leads to considerate action, they are nothing." Lowell's words were apparently read and absorbed by many of his contemporaries. In the fall of 1860 Americans elected a tall, awkward looking, but substantive speaker who was a very thoughtful candidate for president – Abraham Lincoln!

It is interesting to note that in the election of 1860 one of Lincoln's Democratic rivals was the same elegant speaker, U.S. Senator Stephen Douglas from Illinois, whom Lincoln had earlier debated in his losing bid for that Senate seat. Fortunately for Lincoln and the country, the southern Democrats had split from the northern Democrats and ran their own candidate who split the vote, thus allowing Lincoln to win the presidency without getting a majority of the vote.

While communications have improved greatly during my lifetime, the information we absorb has not always lived up to that improvement. In the presidential election of 1952, it was reported that the Democratic candidate, Illinois Governor Adlai Stevenson, was approached by an enthusiastic supporter who said she knew he would win because all of the educated and thinking voters were supporting him. Stevenson replied that while that was all well and good, it would not be nearly enough, because to win he needed a majority. I think any candidate could very well make that same statement today.

About Experience
Another name for education

Suppose you are an army officer during a war. You and your troops are about to enter the combat zone against battle-hardened soldiers. If you were in that situation and you could choose between two groups of people to lead, who would you be more likely to select: A group of raw recruits or a group of seasoned veterans? I suspect you would most certainly choose the latter.

Education and experience are parallel paths leading to the same place: knowledge. Interestingly, one is not always a substitute for the other. In many situations it is the experience that is preferred; while in others your experience may blind you to what you have been taught.

It takes an incredible amount of education and experience to become a successful test pilot. No matter how much formal education you may have, you will not be able to fly a developmental or experimental aircraft to evaluate its performance. That requires experience. On the other hand, you may be the most experienced pilot in the country, but without being educated about the aerodynamics, avionics, and idiosyncrasies of the new aircraft's design, your experience with other planes could lead you to do something that could get you killed.

Many pilots have experienced the sensation of sitting blindfolded in a chair while it is rapidly twisted and turned into unusual positions. Then the person in the chair is asked what direction he or she is facing when the movement stops. The person rarely gives a correct answer. Their body may tell them they are sitting upright when they are actually upside down.

Experience may not always provide the correct answer and, therefore, is not a complete substitute for what can be learned from books. I could also argue that education is part of the experience process.

I like to think of formal education as climbing to the top of a mountain and looking down into the valley at what can be seen and heard; then looking toward the horizon and up at the sky; then looking farther to the right and left to examine the entire vista. It is an eye-opening and broadening process. If you stay up there long enough, it will get dark and a whole new field of view – a small portion of the universe – will reveal itself for exploration.

When you pursue knowledge in any field of endeavor you first struggle to reach a point of understanding that then allows you to perceive new insights. The more you survey the scene using that newly acquired insight, the more you can recognize and understand what your senses are telling you. If you stick with it long enough, whole new worlds will be added to your base of knowledge.

What I am saying is that there are several dimensions involved in obtaining your experience base. You need to be critical about what you think you are learning as well as what you experience.

My mother frequently reminded me that you can't tell a book by its cover. What she meant was that we often are presented with something that appears to be one thing, but it is really something else. You encounter this in situations where someone wants to get your attention in order to have you review a product or service. Newspapers and magazines use this technique all the time. The headline is designed to pique your interest and get you to read the story. It is a common practice in advertising. Be aware that this method is used in other ways that are not so straightforward.

Television and radio news programs, including *Meet the Press, Face The Nation,* and *All Things Considered,* frequently feature guests who are considered experts about whatever topic is being discussed. The moderators introduce these experts as a fellow or analyst at a well-known think tank or the author of a recent book to enhance their credibility. The hosts explain, for example, that "Ralph Smirdly is a permanent fellow at the American Heritage Foundation." It always sounds very impressive. The experts expound on the subjects with great authority to support their positions and opinions. You are led to believe that the experts have conducted thorough and objective analyses of all the available information and are basing their conclusions or their exhaustive research. That, however, may not always be the case. Perhaps the book is different from its glossy cover.

I want to alert you to the fact that many of these institutions identified as "think tanks" are really what I call "fish tanks." What I mean is that the so-called "experts" begin their analyses with the conclusions they want to present and then they go fishing through the available data for the right information to support those conclusions. Many think tanks have been established by special interest groups or corporations for the sole purpose of advancing an economic or a political agenda. Many have been extremely well endowed by wealthy individuals or interest groups who recognize that, with the proliferation of network and cable news programs; there is a near frantic search for content. Therefore, why not have their points of view presented under the guise of an intellectual review of the data by highly educated people with loads of impressive sounding credentials?

This whole area has been compounded by the fact that some of the wealthy interest groups and corporations have substantial influence with the owners of the media outlets.

I believe it is worth your while to make sure you understand the sources of your information, especially the information you need to make important decisions, and that you should be curious enough to try to determine what may be the motivation behind those sources. The introduction of this kind of influence into our information flow has certainly added an element of frustration to the equation. Experience is frequently the best way to sort it all out.

About People
People vary as much inside as outside

We have many different physical features in our family alone: blond, red, brown, black, and grey hair; blue, brown, and hazel eyes; tall, short, and skinny bodies; big feet and little feet. The list goes on. Thankfully, the variety throughout the world defies the imagination. Just imagine how boring it would be if everyone on Earth looked just like you. OMG!

Interestingly enough, while we are all different, we spend much of our time in the company of people who are a great deal like us. We seek out people with common interests. It started early when we attended school or even during family gatherings. We were drawn to people who were easy to relate to and who we could converse with comfortably.

As you ventured into the world and participated in more activities, you again got to know people who liked to do similar things such as exercising, skiing, golfing, studying, shopping, observing, and playing team sports. As you migrated toward people you were comfortable being around, you also separated yourself from people you were not comfortable with. You began to observe common traits involving different groups of people. You became more and more biased in your thinking and were influenced by the ideas and people who you generally agreed with. In a nutshell, you were subjected to considerable influences because of your chosen environment.

Technology is facilitating this phenomenon just as it has facilitated almost every other area of human endeavor. With your smart phones and computers you can now tailor the types of information you receive daily. You can exist in an isolated world of your own choosing. Now everyone can be cast in the image of what used to be called "the mad scientist," someone who is totally absorbed in one narrow interest and unabashedly expresses his or her passion for it. Now, of course, this kind of focus is not limited to scientific persuasions. It may be a fixation on certain teen idols.

I caution you to guard against such narrow concentrations! Please try hard to approach the world and the people you meet with an open mind. Let every day be part of a lifelong learning experience. To be successful in most enterprises requires that you develop an expertise and be able to effectively use that knowledge. But that does not mean you should exclude other information and influences.

As you reach out to the world around you and pursue different areas of knowledge, you will discover an amazing thing about all of the apparently ordinary people you meet. Many of them are truly extraordinary once you get to know them! We are surrounded by extraordinary people. How many times have you met people who seemed so ordinary, only to become fascinated by what they had accomplished or by their breadth of knowledge after you spent some time with them and began to get some insight into what they're doing? I have been privileged to meet many incredible individuals during my great adventure. What I have learned is that we have the same interests, worry about the same things, and share similar aspirations no matter what country or continent we live in. We all want our children to be healthy and live rich and rewarding lives. And we frequently seem to share common biases within our cultures.

One area of human development that has been with us since the dawn of the hunter-gatherer civilizations is the blatant bias against women. The time has long since passed when men's muscles have been critical to the survival of our species. Women have been abused, battered, assaulted, even killed, and consistently denied opportunities and prevented from realizing their dreams and aspirations throughout all of human history. They are still being denied equal opportunities almost everywhere to some extent, including civilized countries such as our own. That needs to stop, and you need to help make it stop.

Graduating to Adulthood

Time after time, when women have been given the opportunities, they have excelled, frequently equaling the productivity of men and often outperforming them. History is full of examples. Much has been written about the leaders of the ancient world and their achievements, but not many were shrewder or more capable at negotiations than Cleopatra. She persuaded two of the most powerful men in the Roman Empire to do her bidding, and she did it by using her brains rather than her sex. Both Julius Caesar and Mark Antony accepted her as their equal. Most of us are under the impression that she was little more than a clever and conniving harlot. History, however, is written by the victors, and it was ultimately the Roman elite who wrote most of what we know about Ancient Egypt and Cleopatra. Clearly, those in power who came after her did not like being upstaged by a woman.

Queen Elizabeth I of England, if rated for accomplishments during her reign, would certainly be ranked among the top ten best monarchs in history and probably among the top three. Hers was an extraordinary reign during which a bankrupt country became a world superpower and remained so for three hundred and fifty more years. She was an incredible CEO.

The modern world has witnessed many women on the international stage who have demonstrated all of the competence and skill of any peer, male or female: Golda Meir as the fourth prime minister of Israel; Margaret Thatcher as prime minister of the United Kingdom; and, more recently, Angela Merkel as chancellor of Germany and Hillary Clinton as secretary of state of the United States. These are but a few examples that profoundly demonstrate the abilities of women to perform admirably under the most difficult and demanding circumstances.

As a student of history, I have spent a great deal of time studying how various leaders and political bodies have affected our existence over time. So much war and destruction, so much intolerance, so much greed and envy, so many male-dominated egos seeking through bluster and battle to feed their narcissistic need for power and domination.

I can't help but wonder what our world would be like if women had been in control during the last three thousand years or even the last three hundred years. And I can't help but share my bias. I have concluded that if women had been running the world we would have had more negotiations concerning peoples' grievances and much more peace and fewer wars. I believe healthcare would better serve the citizens in need and that people would have more access to education. It may sound utopian, but please think about it.

What would we have to lose? Men have been in charge for all these years all over the world. Why not place more trust in our women? Could they do worse? Actually, I think it would be best to have both men and women participating as equals. I do think the United States Congress would be a much more civil and productive place if that were the case.

I think that because women have been denied their proper place for so long in so many cultures they have had to learn to adapt to those circumstances. It seems to me – and I acknowledge it is without any empirical evidence to back it up – that not only are women better negotiators but they are more patient in dealing with people. They have practiced incredible tolerance in so many areas and continue to achieve only incremental progress in their quest for total equality. I am waiting for the day when a woman wins a marathon in which men are competing. I am told that such a thing is impossible because woman do not have the physical strength and stamina to accomplish such a feat. But, to me, they have already demonstrated that they have just as much endurance as men, and I am convinced that I will witness a marathon won by a woman during my lifetime. If it were not for the recent domination of the Kenyans, it might already have happened.

Much of my bias in favor of women comes from observing my mother. Mom lived to be almost ninety-two, and her mind was fully active the whole time. She was born in 1916 and spent her teenage years during the Roaring Twenties and the Great Depression of the thirties. She was married in May 1936, and she gave birth to her first child – me – in January 1938. My father was unemployed at that time, and my mother would live in poverty and endure a cumulative ninety months of pregnancies, resulting in ten children and two miscarriages, during her lifetime. Yet, she always smiled when she greeted people. Being poor did not mean she was not rich in knowledge or friends. My mother showed a toughness of mind and body that I am hard pressed to emulate.

We have already explored the concepts that everyone is unique and that you should be able to deal with almost everyone as equals. However, there are people who seem to find pleasure in causing other people pain and aggravation. Look at the thousands of computer viruses and programs that have been generated to disrupt other people's business and personal activities and to invade their privacy. While all of that is annoying and, many times, costly as well, it is insignificant compared to the harm that leaders of nations can inflect on so many people who are caught up in their domains. While I suspect that you will not have to deal with any of these leaders, you will have to deal with individuals who intend to do you harm on some level. One of the best defenses you can have is your own awareness that these people exist and, therefore, that some thinking is required on your part to avoid being too naive in your dealings with them.

Shortly after I was married, I read in a newspaper that the crown prince of some African country was hospitalized nearby after he had suffered a fainting spell while on his way to visit a local college. "Wow," I thought, wouldn't it be interesting to meet and talk with him. I impulsively drove to the hospital and actually got into his room and met him. He had a small canvas bag, a very colorful robe, a necklace, and some bracelets. That was it. No assistants. Nothing else. He thanked me for visiting and described his country and told of how his father was the chief of a large tribe and who had great wealth and many wives. He further explained that he had just obtained permission from his doctors to leave the hospital and was about to go to the train station where he would wait for a few hours before catching a train to New York. I told him I would be glad to drive him to the train station. Better yet, if he had a few hours to kill I would be honored if he would come to my humble apartment and we could have something to eat, and then I would take him to the station.

My wife was dumbfounded when I walked into our apartment with this gentleman. Here I was, accompanied by a tall, thin, and very black man in a brightly colored robe who she had never seen before; and I was asking her to set another plate at the table. We ate and I then took him to the train station and said good-bye.

The next day the newspapers ran a story about a confidence man who had a serious medical condition and who had skipped out on the Heywood Hospital in Gardner, Massachusetts, without paying his bill. Evidently he had been traveling through many states posing as an African crown prince. I had been conned hook, line, and sinker! That was one of the most memorable lessons I ever learned about dealing with people I did not know. You can probably imagine how many good laughs my family and friends had at my expense about the episode we now call "The Clown Prince Affair."

You should be aware of the fact that other people are not going to share your experiences or your values. What you value may mean little or nothing to others. On the other hand, you may not have the slightest appreciation for someone else's deeply cherished ideas or guiding principles. Like so many other areas, dealing with other people can be a complex situation at many levels.

About Health
Healthy minds and bodies require hard work

Even though we are born with all of the right body parts and operational software, we have never been able to function wholly on automatic pilot. From the time we are born, we need constant care and feeding. The basic question is whether that care and feeding is performed solely for survival or with the idea of nourishing our whole body and mind.

Whatever the case may be, there is undoubtedly room for improvement!

One of the biggest advantages of living in these times is that there is little mystery about what constitutes a healthy lifestyle. Numerous studies have been conducted, sampling large groups of people, to identify the most effective behavior required to sustain a long life and to experience good health throughout it. What you are is just as important as who you are.

I can testify to the fact that when you are young your body is far more tolerant than it is as you grow older. In your youth you can go longer without sleep and endure greater physical challenges, such as imbibing too much alcohol.

I can also testify to the fact that any damage you do to your body during your youth can have severe consequences in your later years. I cannot tell you how many times dermatologists have cut precancerous growths out of my body. They were most likely caused by overexposure to the sun when I was a younger man. My nose is permanently disfigured from one such procedure. Additionally, I now know that had I improved my diet many years ago, I might not have had to undergo extremely invasive surgery when I was sixty-five to remove my cancerous prostate gland. That same kind of attention to my lifestyle and eating habits might also have kept my esophagus healthy and saved me from the trauma of spending one week in the intensive care unit at the hospital in Abington, Pennsylvania.

You can avoid so many of those future difficulties by taking reasonable steps now. It's hard to modify behavior when you don't realize there's any reason to do so and there are no apparent consequences involved. This is why I hope to appeal to the analytical and logical part of your brain.

We now know there is a correlation between obesity and the incidence of diabetes and various forms of cancer. Obesity greatly increases the odds that a person will develop diabetes. When I worked at Acme Electric in Leominster, Massachusetts, many years ago, the owner of the company was diabetic and under a doctor's care. His eyeglasses got stronger and stronger every time he had his eyes examined until, finally, even when wearing his magnifying glasses, he was legally blind and could not see well enough to perform the everyday tasks required to run his company. By then he had turned over the management reins to his son.

In just a few short years, the owner regressed from living independently to being confined to only the places, such as his home, that he knew by heart. He enrolled at the Perkins School for the Blind to learn Braille and how to navigate with a cane. I drove him to the school, which is close to Boston, and picked him up every week. During those rides he would tell me about the things he was learning, such as how to light a cigarette by first placing a finger on the cigarette's end and then moving the flame to that spot or how to put rubber bands with Braille printing around canned goods to identify the contents. I learned firsthand the extent to which diabetes can impair a person's ability to enjoy life.

Obesity is now known to increase the odds of getting several kinds of cancer. Being obese used to mean that you were extremely heavy. Your percentage of body fat is now considered the most important factor in defining obesity. Ideally, twenty-two percent or less is considered a good fat to body ratio, and anyone over twenty-eight percent is considered obese and at risk of associated health problems.

Graduating to Adulthood

Another area that is not given the attention it needs when we are young is our hearing. Your exposure to loud noises now may cause enormous inconveniences later. I can attest to the fact that constantly wearing hearing aids is not a fun thing to do. It can be a source of embarrassment if you do not understand what is being said to you or do not know that someone is talking to you. It is better to be teased now if you put on ear protectors when you know you will be near something loud than to have to insert hearing aids when you are older. Believe me, you do not want to have to deal with an acute hearing loss. But we live in a noise-polluted world – think motorcycles – and unless you protect yourself from unhealthy levels of sound you could experience hearing problems as you age.

When we are young we do feel that we are pretty much invincible. It really doesn't occur to us that many of the infirmities we see in elderly people could happen to us. That certainly was the case with me! I always had a great deal of enthusiasm and energy which led me to believe I could do anything I wanted without fear of injury or illness. Believe it or not, for as long as I can remember I have been convinced that I will live to be one hundred.

So many events that occur when we are young do impact us later in our lives, and we undertake many of them without thinking about eventual consequences. Doctors studying space medicine have recently found that astronauts who have spent significant amounts of time in zero gravity have developed problems with their eyes and their pituitary glands. Those problems were never anticipated, and doctors are still unsure how to correct the situation. But it is another in a long list of precautions that should lead us to err on the side of avoiding risks when dealing with personal health.

One practical way to guard your health is to keep only healthy foods in your home and to follow a diet that will keep you healthy and strong. Moderate amounts of food and a proper balance of nutrition are considered best. We are fortunate because so much good information is available about healthy eating and quality exercise regimens. As more and more research is concluded, it seems to support the idea that being a vegetarian is definitely a good idea. I'm not going to tell you what to eat, but I am asking you to be particular about your diet and to pay close attention to the sources of your nutrition.

Improved farming techniques and transportation coupled with genetic manipulation of food plants and animals has made it easier to supply consumers with fruits, vegetables, fish, fowl, and animals year round without regard to seasons. Unfortunately, many of these techniques and manipulations have been inserted in our food supply with consequences that are not always adequately understood. Many of the problems that have arisen from similar efforts in the past have required long periods to manifest themselves. The people who are financially rewarded by the introduction of these changes are usually reluctant to recognize potential downsides. I believe that, in time, we will discover significant health issues because of processed foods and some of the chemical additives that facilitate longer shelf life and improve the appearances of fruits and vegetables. Many people already believe there is a growing body of evidence associating these substances with certain types of cancer.

I am not trying to be overly negative about this subject. I just want you to fully understand how important it is to watch yourself and to stay as healthy as you can. That means controlling your weight and staying in good shape. Keeping yourself fit is so rewarding. Believe me, it is a major contributor to a happy, fun-filled life! You owe it to yourself, and to those you love, to safeguard your health and protect what has been described as a temple given to you by God – your body!

About Done
Conclusion

When I started writing this, I had no idea it would evolve into such a lengthy book. I apparently had more on my mind than I realized. Believe it or not, I have actually gone back and shortened sections, and I have omitted some things that I would like to have included in order to keep it to a length you might find time to read.

I know I have presented a smorgasbord of thoughts, opinions, and information for you to consider. But if you take away even a few ideas that will enhance your life and your future, I will have fulfilled my mission.

So let me summarize the essence of what I want to convey in these thoughts for my grandchildren and other young people.

Try to be aware of who benefits from changes in rules and why advocates for change propose them, and seek to understand the possible consequences of such actions. Fear not what others think of you and your exploits. Have the courage of your convictions, stand up for what you believe, and do not let yourself be intimidated. Learn how to effectively communicate with people verbally and in writing as well as with your appearance and demeanor. Strive to learn about people and their cultures so you can better understand their values and appreciate what their actions might mean.

You can be quite happy as a leader or follower; but if you lead, lead with purpose and integrity. If you do want to move into a leadership position, understand that it will behoove you to let your actions and your bearing identify you as a person who should be followed. Understand that in most business organizations real leaders are few and far between because most people in management roles are just that – managers, not leaders.

True happiness comes from the effective use of your inner reservoir of infinite love, and I encourage you to spread it about liberally. Focus on maintaining a positive attitude free of anger or grudges. When you love your world and embrace the people in it, the world will love you back and you will be richly rewarded for your efforts. Be sure to always remember that your integrity is your personal currency. It should never be compromised.

It cannot be overemphasized that the judgments you will make will be incredibly important, so choose well when faced with decisions, taking time to understand the consequences including those to your health and well-being. Remember that there is a connection between how you feel and how you behave and that when you are truly happy you will simply radiate. Do as much as you can to keep your body and your mind in top shape with exercise, travel, and intellectual curiosity. And always try to enjoy the journey.

Set both short- and long-term goals, and understand that your values will strongly influence your decisions and the lifestyle you choose to lead.

Be aware of what a unique individual you are and that you determine your own path. No one other than you is ever truly responsible for where you may find yourself; and it is up to you, and only you, to decide where you are going to go from that point in your life.

I hope by now that you fully appreciate that wealth is accumulated over a lifetime. You will need to establish and maintain a lifetime of disciplined saving to accumulate your own wealth. Like your personal well-being, wealth contributes enormously to your level of enjoyment and your relationships with others.

Take time to understand the people around you, and be inquisitive enough to learn why people choose to live the way they do. And be grateful that you can live the way you want to because you have the great fortune of living in the phenomenally diverse and culturally rich United States of America. Be very much involved in your democratic form of government, and do as much as you can to protect it for others as well as for yourself.

I have a special message for you women. The time for you to insist on a seat at the table has long since passed. You should be there. As for you men, it is only good manners to move over and make room for the women. And I remind you once again to follow a path of good health by constantly exercising your body and your brain.

I have always been impressed with this statement by former Notre Dame football coach Lou Holtz: "Ability is what you're capable of doing. Motivation determines what you do. Attitude determines how well you do it."

I hope that what I have written will alert you to situations that you should avoid or at least increase your sensitivity so you will more quickly grasp the implications of your actions as well as those of people around you. I feel obligated to remind you not to think of me as a person with only a few faults. That is not the case. But I do try to do good and add value to our world, and I sincerely want to have a positive impact on your world as well.

My deepest desire is for all of you to experience lives that are more rewarding than mine; that are enriched with great adventure, happiness, a sense of achievement, satisfaction and, always, peace of mind.

I sincerely hope that this collection of thoughts has been valuable to you, and I solicit your comments and critiques. I'm most interested in what parts you think can be shortened or omitted as well as those that you think could be enhanced or better explained. As you know, many of my grandchildren are too young to appreciate this book right now, but perhaps with your help we can improve it so it will be of even greater use to them when they are ready to take their place in the world.

As the Vulcan Mr. Spock of the TV series *Star Trek* would say: "Live long and prosper."

About the author:

Born during the Great Depression in central Massachusetts, Peter Gravelle is the oldest of ten children. He began to develop his passion for reading and a lifetime of learning in a two-room schoolhouse.

After furthering his education at Clark University, Suffolk University Law School, and Dartmouth College, Peter rose through the financial and executive ranks of some of the best-managed companies in America – Raytheon, Tyco, and Eaton – and ultimately became president of Kysor Industrial. He is also a member of the Massachusetts Bar Association and a multiengine-rated pilot.

Upon retirement, Peter immersed himself in creating small businesses and consulting for domestic manufacturing firms. He has learned from them all and is passionate about sharing his experiences with others – especially with young people on the brink of adulthood. That was his reason for writing this book.

Peter and his wife Mary have been married for more than fifty years and have traveled to more than fifty countries. They have raised four children and are the proud and very involved grandparents – "Grampy" and "Nonna" – of twelve grandchildren from five to twenty-five years old. The couple resides in Massachusetts or Florida when they are not traveling.

Peter has written poetry, short stories, and blogs. *Graduating to Adulthood* is his first book.

Made in the USA
Lexington, KY
11 August 2013